THE
GREAT
BRITISH
WRITE OFF

The Power Of The Pen

Edited By Donna Samworth

First published in Great Britain in 2016 by:

Forward Poetry
Coltsfoot Drive
Peterborough
PE2 9BF
Telephone: 01733 890066
Website: www.forwardpoetry.co.uk

FOREWORD

Here at Forward Poetry our aim has always been to provide a bridge to publication for unknown poets and allow their work to reach a wider audience. We believe that poetry should not be exclusive or elitist but available to be accessed and appreciated by all.

Our latest competition 'The Great British Write Off' was created to celebrate the writing talent we have here in the UK. We invited poets and authors to write either a poem, a short story or even an extract from a novel that showcases their ability. The result is an entertaining collection of creative writing that expresses and communicates thoughts, feelings and ideas on a multitude of subjects.

Whether you prefer humorous rhymes, poignant odes or a thrilling short story, there is something in these pages to suit every reader's taste. We are very proud to present this anthology and we are sure it will provide entertainment and inspiration for years to come.

CONTENTS

Karen Adela Barnes	122	Anthony Bryce	184
Brian Francis Kirkham	124	Lionel Etherington	185
Michael Vickery	125	Brad Evans	186
Jane Air	126	Cheryl Vallely	187
Robert Shooter	128	Andrew Evzona	188
Zak Patrick Parsons	129	Darren Halladay	189
Graham Hayden	130	Agnes Brookes	190
Catherine Wilson	131	Ruth Miser	191
Valerie Sutton	132	Jennifer O'Gorman	192
Charlotte Ransley	134	Janet Vernon	193
Tolulope Akinyemi	135	Kathy Rawstron	194
Gary Moss	136	Norman Dickson	195
Eva J K Skarviken	138	Hannah Derbyshire	196
Temi Daike	140	Alex Oleksy	197
Philip Rugg	141	Asma Khatun	198
Danielle Harris	142	Nigel Mellor	199
Vivien Foster	144	Pauline Uprichard	200
Kevan Taplin	145	Nicola Penistone	201
Delores James	146	Victoria McAnerney	202
Olivia Gillespie	148	Becky Bishop	203
Susan Vowden	149	Kerri Madders	204
Diane Ashman	150	Christabel Samuel	205
Peter Taylor	151	Vivienne Doncaster	206
Sarah Safraz	152	Lee Blunt	207
Ashley A Burnside	153	Laura Aimee	208
Philip Caveney	154	Rob Dunsford	209
Burgess Jay Barrow	156	Tanya Silva	210
Victoria Sands	158	Paul Mein	211
Gregory McDowell	160	Sheffphil	212
Gillian Garwood	161	Felicity Milne	213
Andy Brister	162	Denis Bruce	214
Paulina Bawiec	164	Barbara Coward	215
David Dixon	166	Sonya Hussain	216
Swati Gupta	168	Brian Weston	217
Pat Salisbury-Ridley	169	Maura Guerin	218
Shelley Foreman	170	Barry Bradshaigh	219
Simon Day	172	Victoria Penn	220
David Satherley	174	Abigail Quigley	221
Jenny Proom	176	Audrey D'souza	222
Adrian McRobb	178	Wayne Barrow	223
Phil Brooks	180	Adam Cook	224
Tia-Louise Way	182	sweetwater	225
Peter Stephenson	183	Holly Thwaites-Bee	226

Three Years Too Late

You silently abandoned me without a single word
During three secluded years nothing had I heard
Then quite randomly from you, I receive a text
Three years too late...
Am I meant to be impressed?
No offered apologies or words of explanation
Nor feelings of regret for three years' deprivation
Now you tell me you love me
And that you made a dreadful mistake
Yet to rectify this wrong
A text is the only action you can take?
Three years of lonely Valentines have gone
Did you send a bouquet, card or a single red rose?
No, not a flippin' one!
All I get is a text inviting me for a drink
A little more diligence my dear
Long overdue I think!
Three more birthdays have passed
Making me older and more wise
A gesture other than a text is required
How could you not realise?
Why now after three years' absence
Do you want to see me again?
A question I keep texting you back
The answer to which,
I'm still struggling to attain
Since we parted there's been no other
Likewise
You defensively reciprocate...
So why now finally choose to contact me
When it's three bloody years too late!

Paula Holdstock

Help For Heroes?

The ultimate sacrifice!
If it's required
They are told it's their duty
Programmed, and hot wired

Yet - I see 'Help for Heroes'
On the TV again
'Please pledge, just one pound
Better still - make it ten'

The *limbless*
Disfigured
And *mentally scarred*
Exist
In *their nightmares*
Forever,
now marred

While astute politicians
Stand and preach, in their suits
Their careers first and foremost
In their list, of pursuits

Unwilling to care
For young lives that are broken
Relying on charity
As a blackmailing token

'The fight is for *freedom!*'
Sound the heavenly choirs
Yet - justice and truth
Are restrained by the *liars*

Who evoke plain ol' charity
To strike at our heart
With honour - unknowing
We play our own part

In the game - where our lives
Are abundant and cheap
Where the broken survivors
Lay piled in a heap

To condone this monstrosity
Is the depth of depravity
Where judgement is blinded
Where there's a lack of morality

So, I simply ask - quietly
With no wish, to patronise
Please pause, for a while
Please, open your eyes

To supposed, *'Help for Heroes'*
Which should leave us shamefaced
To be judged by our children
As fools, and disgraced.

Archie Macdonald

My First, Your Second

My love, I need to tell you something,
But how do I say the words?
I want to have your baby,
But this won't be your first.

Anything I'd do for little man,
As a mum would love her own,
And I would lay down my own life,
For him, he's in my heart.

But when the time does come around,
And my tummy starts to grow,
Will you be as in love,
As the time you were before?

Will they all be as amazed
And will it be the same?
For those two there with their first,
As we will with our own.

Will it be exciting
As I know it won't be new?
Preparing for all that lies ahead,
And preparing for all the poo!

Reading books and learning tricks,
You've taught it all before,
I know you'll love us till the end,
But will it be a bore?

What about the nappies,
The ups, the downs, the lot?
You're prepared for what might happen,
But then again I'm not.

My love, I need to ask you something,
But it's breaking my heart to say,
That when we have our own baby,
Will it be the same?

Roseannah Collison

A Unique Lady

Let me tell you about someone, who in my life has been so dear
Although, sadly for me, I should also say that she's no longer here

So very many qualities, but not completely without fault
She always handled with aplomb the cards that she'd been dealt

A possessor of rare beauty, both on the inside and the out
A turner of heads, a winner of hearts, of that there is no doubt

So full of dreams when younger, not all of which came true
But hope resided in her heart, even when she felt so blue

Loved and admired by young and old, she really was the best
Funny, kind, she knew her own mind, and your patience, she
could test

Strong and wise, but fragile too - an enigma to many, for sure
Passionate, proud and frequently feisty, someone you
couldn't ignore

Full of advice, she knew what to say, and had known her share
of sadness
Not one to surrender, she always came through, and did enjoy
great gladness

Now she's gone, and time moves on, though nothing is quite
the same
This world is better for her having been here, such an
extraordinary dame

She was an inspiration to all, who I loved with all my heart
I could tell you of so many memories, but I wouldn't know where
to start

A truly colossal presence in my life, quite unlike any other
Words cannot convey how lucky I feel that this lady was
my mother.

Jenny Quigley

Child Of Its Time

Born in the wrong time
In the wrong family
It's not his fault
He should be in school
Not doing a man's job
Experiencing the sweat and grime

Should be with his mates
Outside, there beyond the factory gates
Childhood ebbing with the sweat dripping
Young lungs breathing in the fumes

Trudges home at the sound of the bell
Already walking like the adults and coughing like hell
Father pats his back saying, 'A good day's work.'
He can barely walk, let alone smile
As he walks home the last mile

Mother greets them with a smile but looks at the lad
No choice to work, no other way
Her smile looks so sad

The extra money puts food on the table
Got to take Dad's mantle the way he's going
Because soon he won't be able
Food is up, they're grateful but isn't yummy
But at least it'll fill an empty tummy

When the food is gone he can go outside
Whatever the weather, sunny or bleak
He grabs the tired remains of his childhood
Playing ball, fighting or hide-and-seek
He doesn't belong here like so many others
But he's a child of then, a child of its time.

Karl Hawkins

Her Love For You

Her love for you swims oceans
Just to look into your eyes,
It peers over the precipice
Without fear of its demise.

You've always been her heartbeat;
A coursing pulse of red,
Great rivers of it just for you
Resounding in her head.
Her shoes of scarlet ribbons
Trailing softly in her wake,
Dancing, twirling, just for you,
Lit up by a sparkling lake.

This lake of deep blue nothing
Makes her feel so very small,
But your lightning lights her tropical
Until she has no fears at all.
A cobalt flash runs through her eyes,
Which used to sit so grey.
She knows that she will love you
Until they take the skies away.

She wore a golden wedding dress
And sang the night away,
This was her coronation;
She became your queen that day.
And as the sun was setting,
Yellow, bold against the sky,
She swore that she would love you
For long after she died.

Ruth Cooke

The Ocean And Its Memories

The crescent shape of the moon rests on the sky.
The reflection beams on down from way up high.
The ocean bed all silent and all is still.
The waves slowly rolling out and then back to a standstill.

The stars flickering in the distance of the midnight blue.
Like miniature glowing candles they break through.
The wide space of water and sky give an illusion of never-ending.
With the hour of daytime forever impending.

The velvet sky full of stars kiss the ocean below.
As the water slowly comes to life and begins to flow.
The waves grow more and more with each crash.
On the stones and rocks they hit hard and smash.

The sun now sitting very low in the sky.
And birds begin to ascend and fly.
The start of the day and what's to come.
All begin with the biggest star, the ever-burning sun.

The day gets warmer and the ocean reflects the clear blue.
With no clouds in the sky the sun can cut through the water too.
Many do embrace the ocean to cool down from the heat.
When all is over the timeline does repeat.

The memories that are made will be held in an instant.
Locked in the ocean ready for recapture even when it feels
distant.
The memories roll out with waves and come back with the sun.
What secrets those waves hold are all a lot and endless fun.

Shannon Fountaine

The Journey

Sometimes we have to journey a long way to travel a
short distance.
We also find this hard to understand!

Patience I am told is a virtue but this is not something that
I have.
Everything is out of my control.

It's not being able to move forward, that I found to be such a
strain.
Days turn into weeks, then months into years.
What ifs, maybes, when, why and how?
Trust me, this is not a nice place to be.

I guess it's the not knowing that I struggle with the most.
Not being the most positive person I am told, does not help.
Is this not a way to protect oneself?

I wait for the telephone to ring; will it be good news? I
ask myself.
So many questions inside my head, I try so very hard to close them
down but still they keep coming.

The sheer frustration of having no control is driving
me crazy.
Waiting for others to do what's needed so that I am able to move
a little further, to achieve my goal.
But for now I must continue my journey and hope that whatever
may happen, it was meant to be.

Janice Freeman

George

Some years ago I made a friend - a man I grew to know,
He welcomed me into his life and happy I was so,
We bonded over cups of tea and stories from the past,
So many treasured memories, the time would go so fast.

Born and raised in London, joined the navy at 18,
The uniform he wore with pride, he kept it all pristine,
He came from next to nothing but he made himself a life,
He had four lovely children after marrying his wife.

Valerie, Malcolm, Wendy, then baby Paulene came along,
He didn't beat around the bush, he'd tell you if you were wrong,
He liked to do the gardening, kept his gardens always nice,
He'd turn his hand to anything, never pausing to think twice.

He loved to read his factual books, his knowledge was so vast,
He also liked to tell a joke, even when I saw him last,
In March it was his birthday and he turned the big 'nine-o',
We all sang songs together, now it seems so long ago.

I often called him Grandad which he didn't seem to mind,
He knew I loved him dearly as he always was so kind,
But now it's time to bid farewell to George, my dearest friend,
I wish you peace in Heaven, George, and all my love I'll send.

Veronica Ingram

Procrastination Station

I don't know what to tell you
because I don't want to upset you
but I've been sat here doing nothing
though I'm pretty sure it's close to something
in the back of my mind
wrap me up in cellophane
so my feeble brain
can unwind
and I won't feel the rain.

Shit!
an approaching landslide
of formaldehyde,
cyanide
It
won't make me cry
though rather die
and if that gets me gold or silver then I don't mind.

Then they'll be around
me like flies
but I'll use pesticide
and that's bound
to keep them at bay
away
from the prize
my literary gold mine.

Argh! I need a break
from this limbo state

a holiday
getaway
skinny dipping in the sun
I prefer this foray
into the waves
but the naked truth it starts to chill my bum
get your ass back into gear
is all I can hear
passing a parasol to the sun.

I take propanolol
spray aerosol
create a cloud of mist and hide
calm my nerves of critical suicide
escape the plight
of my situation
halted at Procrastination station
I need to book a flight
cos it's the end of the train track
and the only way is back
but I won't be breaking mine.

You can't force me
to continue the story
unless you force-feed me
like a suffragette
but in the tube
instead of food
you'll put words
then I'll forget
how this feels like a test
and make progress on this unwritten turd.

Emmeline Pankhurst
hunger strike -
the worst
but now I burst
with words
they keep rollin'
like Fred Durst
it's absurd
a hole-in-
one
a painful procedure
for a vocabulary retriever
a sickening seizure
never to be undone.

I stop and ask myself: what's this all for? The vote?
a part of me just wants the choke
please can
you throttle my self-abasing humour
it's like a tumour
malignant and chasing the gun.

Give me morphine on a drip
and I'll pip
you to the post
but only as your ghost-
writer
credit received in the afterlife

but that'll be too late, bring on the laughter
at my struggle and strife
I deserve a BAFTA
for the fame I bring to your life.

I'm going through an identity crisis
and in spite of this
I have received great feedback
on work I have previously done
yet here I sit, slack
and chew gum
title and nothing else staring back at me
on an otherwise blank screen
like a spleen
bursting at the seams
and weighing a ton
please don't take away from me what I haven't yet written.

And so I'll search through my Google searches
stalk an acquaintance I haven't seen in ages
look up the smallest animals
a list of worldwide massacres
make toast
and coast
along
on indulgent tendencies
through social media and WikiLeaks
caught in the never-ending web so strong.

David Hanlon

A Song For The Melancholy

When we were little kids
We had these unrealistic aspirations,
Thought we'd grow up to all be pilots
Or some kind of awesome artists,
But with age comes decimation
Of all the things you thought you'd be
And now you're trapped inside of this,
Your half-hearted reality.

The birds are deafening
Their bitter sweet tunes are telling me
That somewhere in this life
Are all the things we used to strive to be,
Our dreams are still existing
The spark, it is still beating
It's just that everything we want
Keeps moving further away.

So instead, we'll let you play dress-up
We'll be the puppets you make up
Be parts of your play and your theatre
But you won't cast us as part of your main feature.

We'll forget we ever had dreams and
Hopes of where we'd like to be that now
Will unfortunately never see the light of day,
And we will carry on existing
Simply doing what's expected
Because no one will ever notice that
Inside our souls are crying because
Our hopes and dreams are dying.

We're blinded by our fantasies
Of happy ever after
We've been brainwashed by the
Fairy tales society used to tell
And now we're lost within our minds
Trying to make sense of
This mess that we call life.

If you think you missed a crossroads
And you're thinking this is it
Just take yourself a minute
To sit and have a think
Of Alice, in the forest when
She was lost, alone, afraid
But then she made it out alive
In the end she was strong and brave.

You might have to battle demons
You might have to battle queens
But if the will to live is strong enough
You can battle anything.
When you're sitting on the ground
And looking up towards the sky
You might realise deep, deep down inside
You really want to die.
That's when it's most important
For you to remember this;
The darkness you see inside of you
To us, doesn't exist.

If you listen to the silence
It's sure to drive you insane
Because the silence, it is ignorant
It's all inside your brain.

Just take yourself a minute
To sit and have a think
About the reasons you are here
Standing on the brink
Ready to take the leap
Into the great beyond
Is it really reason enough
For you to always be gone.

All the people that you'd hurt
Is it really worth the rage?
With everybody blaming you
For causing all this pain.
If you were dying anyway
Would you still starve your brain
Of love and lust and oxygen?
Trust me, it's not the same.

It's really not as bad as you think.

The future isn't set in stone
You guide it to its source
Like rivers, meandering
Down throughout the valleys
If you want to reach the ocean
You just need to change your course.

Try to believe that you
Are capable of change
And you can be with Alice
From the cradle to the grave,
Everything will have a way
Of working out just fine
Just take your future by the balls
And make your future yours.

S J Anderson-Potter

Glory To The Father

Glory to the Father, glory to the Son
Glory to the Spirit, glory to the One,
Glory to God Almighty, up in Heaven above,
Glory to our Lord for giving us His love.

Glory to the Father, glory to the Son,
Glory to the Spirit, Glory to the One,
Praise the Lord in Heaven, praise Him most high,
Give your praise to our Lord way up in Heaven's sky.

Glory to the Father, glory to the Son
Sing out your praises to the Holy One,
Raise your voices, raise your voices high
Sing your praises up to Him on high.

Thank the Lord in Heaven for giving us this day,
Thank the Lord in Heaven for each bright new day,
Glory to the Father, glory to the Son,
Glory to His Spirit for He is the One.

Roy Muir

The Denial

The man who climbed the mountain
To look in God's right eye
Was eager to discover
A deity to deny

And at the topmost spur of rock
He stood and he beheld
The misdemeanours of his life
In sin he had excelled

He could not ask forgiveness
For of him he knew not
In desperation flung himself
Into he knew not what

'Twas God alone who saw him fall
Who watched his body roll
Who came and stood beside it
To lead away his soul.

Robert Stevens

Lies

Don't forget
Do not let
My body
Lie and cheat you

Remember you first
Were a liar and a cheat

Do not misread
The arching of my back
For the rebuilding
Of a bridge
That you alone
Burnt down

Do not mishear
My whisper in your ear
As a renewal of vows
Spoken
And broken
By you

Don't think that
Just because
We are
Once again
Wrapped up in these sheets
That you still have me
Wrapped around
Your finger

My feet upon your shoulders
Should not be
Misconstrued as
A sign
That I continue to bend at your will

Right now
I may be on my back
My toes
Pointing towards the skies
But your stars
Will never be in my eyes
Again

Me
On my knees
This time
Does not indicate
That I still pray at your alter
In worship
Of you

This sweat
Of my body
On your body
Should not be mistaken
For
The tears
That I once cried
When I
Cared

I am just
A creature of habit
You are my old habit
And old habits die hard

But with Will
Habits die

And I know that
I said it the last time
But honestly
This is the last time

So do not let
The lies of my body
As we lie here together
Lie
And cheat you

Because I cannot forget

That you first

Were a liar
And a cheat.

Elle Dionne

Facebook Fake

What is a 'like' really?
Behind the lies, the 'oh so nearly',
Why does she always lie?
Being herself no one sees eye to eye,
Why does she make the bad seem good?
For 'likes' of course, I knew she would.
Why so many 'likes' on her pic?
Boobs and bum out, makes me sick!

What is the perfect picture profile?
A selfie taken, pout, don't smile!
Don't show my stomach or my thighs
I need them to believe my lies,
Is perfect being attractive to men?
Full make-up and 'Photoshop' it then,
Why confidence in this fantasy living?
Be careful or you'll end up believing.

Jessie B Benjamin

You Complete Me

I met you when my head was barely above water
My feet hardly aground,
My baggage could have shackled me to all the lost and found.
When cuts ran deep healed by your side,
Tied by the past
By pride,
The pain of loss
The wavering tide that tossed,
I nearly lost
You!
My bride,
Gaining new ground sent from above,
You were my guardian Angel,
The one I married
The One
I truly Love.

Paul Blair

Memories Of Comfort

As I stand looking through the big shop window,
At all the beautiful things that are there on show.
I see a blue wooden cot, just perfect for a sleep,
With a comfy white mattress, two inches deep.
Beside it there is a pram that is fit for a king,
Alongside it, a little blue seat to rock in and swing.
Looking around at all the lovely little toys,
To put a smile on the faces of girls and boys.
All these things would fit nicely in my little box room,
And maybe some murals to brighten the gloom.
Sun shines on the window, inside of the shop is a blare,
I see myself in the reflection, daydreaming as I stand there.
As a mixture of emotions and feelings slowly start to leak
Forming a tear that spills out and slides down my cheek.
My anxiety builds up as my heart hurts and decays
Why did the angels have to come and take my baby away?

Gregory Mcilwaine

Psalm 34: The Happiness Of Those Who Trust In God

'I will bless the Lord at all times;
His praise shall continually be in my mouth.
My soul shall make its boast in the Lord;
The humble shall hear of it and be glad.
Oh, magnify the Lord with me,
And let us exalt His name together'.
Psalm 34:1-3

I will bless the Lord at all times;
His praise shall continually be in my mouth.
Not vain repetitions or empty aesthetics
But He deserves heartfelt expression
Without a doubt

Each breath I inhale is a gift God gave
With every exhale I need to give Him praise
Praise by direct exaltation, words expired from my mouth
Or my living daily, as a living testimony, of the living words
breathed from His mouth

Like 'it is finished', words that denote my salvation is sure
And that I reap a harvest of a work I never started
Eternally indebted because my eternity is secure

My soul shall make its boast in the Lord;
The humble shall hear of it and be glad.

I cannot boast in myself
For I am nothing
Without God the Father, my heavenly Dad

I'm a hidden mess without Him
But in Him, through my mess, I am strong
Thank you Yahweh for showing me Your way
And for Your Spirit's conviction guiding me along

I don't always feel I'm right to represent Him
And my living sacrifice never matches up to His
But He reminds me of the power of His blood
Silences Satan's lies, and whispers that I'm still His

Oh, magnify the Lord with me,
And let us exalt His name together.
Not just in church or on a Sunday
But deposit praise, every day, off the stage, whenever

We can never forget our first love
We must always be in awe of Him
Constantly pressing for His presence
Boldly, as He still removes all our sins

Don't forget where He's brought us from
Keep focusing on where He's taking us to
The joy of trusting in the Lord
Must be seen by the world, in me and you.

RochelleLoRo

Charlie Bubble

I have a little friend,
His name is Charlie Bubble.
He's naughty and mischievous,
And gets me into trouble.
It's only me who sees him,
And I get quite glum.
When I'm getting told off,
For what Charlie Bubble's done.
Why can't Mum believe me
When I say it's Charlie's fault?
I'm sick of getting told off,
When Charlie's not about.
I'm going to get rid of Charlie,
I think I will get by.
I'm going to be a 'grown-up',
And wave Charlie Bubble bye.

Kath Crilly

The Passing Years

It doesn't seem that long ago
You were a baby, I watched you grow
If you fell and grazed your knee
Up you'd get and run to me

It was not long before nursery
You'd love to go,
I was more nervous,
But I didn't let it show

Then time it came for you
To school I sent,
So small you seemed
As off I went

The teenage years arrived all too fast
I told you
The troubled times,
They would not last

When the time comes
For you to fly the nest
As my mum said:
'You can you only do your best!'

And one day,
As we look back at all the laughter and the tears
As we reminisce about the passing years
I hope you know, as my mum said,
That I have tried, I've done my best.

Helen Jennings

On Learning From A Robin, 'Big Boy'

He came in the springtime
The robin we called 'Big Boy'.
Sitting motionless upon the fence,
He fixed his gaze
Then, swiftly swooped,
Gobbling grubs we had provided.

Defying March winds
He returned daily,
Always waiting patiently, on that same fence
Until, one day, there was an urgency about him,
He gathered with purpose
Taking pickings to his young.

June warmth brought a second brood -
And disaster,
Trees felled, torrential rain, hailstones storm!
His nest destroyed.

I found our 'Big Boy'
Alone and desolate, soaked by the rains,
Protecting his nest, with outstretched wings.
A little soldier, uncomplaining, confused,
Mourning the loss of his young.
From that time he made an oasis of our garden;
Waiting silently in solitary bushes
To be found and fed with delicacies he chose.

Yet there were times I despaired...
So dependant,
Did he know he was nearing death?
His breath became shallow, his feathers puffed
And still he came.

Until that day in July,
Bright and perky, I doubted myself
'Are you really 'Big Boy'?' He flew beside me
'Yes my little soldier it is you?'
A recovery short-lived, brief, and indicative of death.
That was the last time I saw our 'Big Boy'... my little soldier...

A death, unexplained, caused grief unexpected
Unprepared, unbelieving, the pain pierced...

I think often of our 'Big Boy'
The trust that existed between us...
The joy of spring and vibrance of his summer...
How he spent his life out for his young
and finally the puffed-up little man I called 'my soldier'.

Yet is not this the way with us all?
The joyous springtime, vibrant summer
Followed by the unexpected rains...
Do not we too spend out our life
For those we love
Before mortality strikes midnight?

Thank you 'Big Boy', our little soldier
Creator's messenger, teacher to the taught
You made our joyful spring and vibrant summer...
And flew from life into eternity.

In our ignorance we breed arrogance
Debating theology, your right to eternity.
Yet God incarnate, born among animals
Cares for each sparrow, embracing creation.

Enclose our Robin 'Big Boy' in your love.

Diana Coutts-Pauling

We Listened To 'Hand In My Pocket'

jagged little collar bone
dishevelled bleached blonde bob
eyes trailed with incongruent
eyeliner

we were fourteen
and Alanis mused on
our future with
a flippant yodel

played harmonica like
it bruised her lips
told us
everything was just fine
fine
fine

on a sunday morning
in a different decade
a different country
I listen to the acoustic version

its sanded-down
guitar riff an apologetic kind
of passion
and I wonder what you
listen to
now that the amps
don't buzz
anymore

Sarah Alderman

Cub

I
While making morning tea, my eye was caught
by the unexpected form;
a lifeless crow-pecked body on the grass.

II
It's not that I'm the squeamish sort
but this stuff's not for city folk,
the business of animal disposal,
the practicalities of carcasses and dirt.
Tentative, I skirt the lawn
and think of tools and processes,
not ready yet to face the thing
hypnotic with the energy of death.

III
I find a spade. I pick a plot
set back amongst the gathered winter leaves.
I strike the ground and it resists
as if unwilling to become a grave.
But I scratch for patient minutes and,
when softer earth's revealed, I dig
and lift and throw and scrape and dig
until I've cut a decent hole
the size of a kitchen basin or a crib.

IV

It was a fight lost hard,
a death died painfully.
Brown blood cakes the claws
and mats the ragged fur along its haunches.
A slash across the trunk displays
a flies' buffet of entrails and gore.
The head is gone, ripped off about the throat
to leave a stump of white protruding spine.

V

I visualise the motion.
Scoop - lift - carry - drop.
Scoop - lift - carry - drop.
But as I plunge and metal meets with flesh
a spasm makes the tail twitch
and I leap back in childish horror.
I hold my breath. I dive again.
The flies, disturbed, take off and stumbling I
can feel the body's weight part from the earth.

VI

Mere inches off the ground,
I stagger with my gruesome egg-and-spoon
towards the grave; but my unsteady hands
and shaking motion cause the corpse to slip
against my planned incisive drop.
The body slides spread-eagled to the hole
and rests in a grotesque come-hither pose.

VII
I sweep the earth back in.
I cover the remains, press down the mud.
I'm half-inclined to say some words.
'Goodnight, sweet fox. Now there's some corner
of a Peckham lawn that is forever yours.'
I dismiss it as absurd.

VIII
I go indoors, reboil the kettle,
think of other things.

Will Green

Twisted Love

Rose petals scattered across the floor
The first thing I see when I walk through the door.
The second is candles spread through the room,
Third I notice the delicate perfume;

Of death that lingers in the air,
And I see the present you've left me tied to a chair,
With pooling blood beneath their feet,
A present like this so thoughtful and sweet.

Following the trail of roses, they lead me straight to you,
My love for you so easy to renew,
As you lay on the bed in nothing but blood,
My heart skips a beat and then continues to thud.

I wrap myself around you covering myself in death,
You breathe me in so we're taking the same breath,
Bodies as one,
Our fun has only just begun.

The rise and fall of a chest,
We go out and we greet our guest,
The screams in the background turn into a beautiful treat,
As we dance along to our new beat.

The stench of death finally whole,
Perfect together we're of the same soul,
We make love at the feet of the one who is now dead,
Fall asleep in each other's arms to wonderful dreams of what's
ahead.

Rowanne Carberry

Hands

I was once told to walk
Through life
With my guard up
Right arm over left
In front of my face
Deflecting any unexpected mysteries
Defending myself; unexposed, hiding
Denying my own freedom

I don't feel this is the way
Both hands out, palms up
Elbow to wrist horizontal
Catching all the mysteries that fall
My way, fighting back
Giving
Receiving
This is the way to approach life
With hopeful hands

Hands that feel the cold
But become warm with that special person
They tremble but instantly stop
When the deal is done and only a hand shake
Made it official.
Hands that show nerves but clench
For determination, confidence and fight

Hands that send pulses of pain through your body
When you have touched a grieving loved one
But their hands embrace their torment
And hold them tightly until hands
Are the only thing left to hold

Hands are powerful
They help seize all the closed books
As they may become adventures
They help fight the fights where
You will be victorious!
They give for the reason of giving
Not to receive
But will receive their comfort
In the hands of another loved one

One whose hands touched your heart
Before your body
Hands that hold your hands
With sweet defeat, tightly
Full of love, hope and warmth

When your hands stop feeling the cold
When there's no need to be afraid and tremble
That's when I know
I've walked through life
Both hands out, palms up
Elbow to wrist, horizontal.

Chloe Wright

Window To The Soul

I believe, so countless experts say
That the eyes are like the window to the soul
Behind which, one can skilfully conceal or reveal
The deepest pools of fragile emotion

Whether looking outward or looking inward
Both the observer and the observed
An empathetic gaze becomes an act of compassion
Conveying without words true benevolence

And so, this new-found epiphany helped me chance
Upon this avenue of altruism and self-kindness
And as I did, I looked with fresh appreciation
And perceived a frail figure in need of love's enveloping

I saw her just a while ago, head bent and eyes downcast
She winced and scarcely turned when I called
Though she tried, she did resolve to face me briefly
With a faint look of recognition

Each ensuing time I observed her passing by
It seemed she hauled her careworn self
As though weighed by a heavy load
Up the steep hill and past my dwelling

I noticed, often behind the security of my pane
No evident encumbrance to weigh her down
Rather, I perceived an invisible burden
An affliction carried within perhaps?

Not carrying her head aloft without cautiousness
Neither did her eyes hold another's gaze too long
But with slumped shoulders
She trudged past to an unknown destination

I found myself drawn, captivated and absorbed
Eagerly, I anticipated her reappearance
Could I glean from her dejected demeanour
The true narrative of her sadness?

My musings and observations became recurrent
Yet her passing by my way was too infrequent
And so, I pondered a painful malady behind her façade
Intrigued, why did she get under my skin so?

At last, I saw her again today!
I hoped I would after her long enigmatic absence
Her gait quicker, her head proud and erect
Fascinated, I speculated what could have caused this change?

Instinctively, I flung wide my window, called out a greeting
'I've missed you... you haven't passed this way in a while'
Decidedly, she turned and smiled while clear green eyes held my
gaze
And I saw myself reflected as I was meant to be.

Julie Alexandra Povall

En Garde

To have thought I tried to be decent,
To be gentle and sweet all the while.
To think you accuse me of misleading,
To find I'm accused of such guile.

Well,

No swear words here are needed,
Though they are sorely kept at bay.
None of my words at all were heeded,
Yet in spite your words did sway.

To tread upon the hand of this writer,
Especially one so kemp and quaint.
Though my person seems ostentatious,
Do you really claim to be a saint?

Hear my echoing voice in your head,
Tear your quarrel, limb by limb.
Brace yourself for the next stanzas,
For the words be certain, and grim.

Many women have come through my life,
Though profess love and hate all the same.
Contradictory to your perceptions,
You have much cause to share their shame.

For when I nested with my lover,
You came with a sniffing, upturned nose.
You were absent through the good times,
But exceptionally present through the lows.

Such words you use as 'plaything',
To describe the string I spun.
Yet not now, or in any youthful year,
Has a 'plaything' ever been less fun.

Another woman that claims she knows me,
Yet slanders me like the rest.
Turns out, I'm not the man she perceived.
Honestly, who'd have guessed?

To speak of love about me,
Though we shared no kiss, no embrace.
Then to call me 'stupid' so bluntly,
Well my dear, I have yet to play my ace.

The inflicted wound would be severe,
Infected worse than a junkie's vein.
Tempt not the blade I sheathe,
Go now, and avoid the pain.

Do not tease to know me.
Do no longer linger and pry.
For the man you see before you,
Hides a demon behind his eye.

Joshua O'Sullivan

Strangford Lough

The six o'clock sun had barely shown
The plastic handle in my hands.
A line of hooks dropped from it -
Down, down into the foam.

I hauled it up then let it sink,
Up and down to make the baits shimmer,
Next to the wheezing engine of
My great-uncle's battle-worn boat.

For an hour I worked as the adults fell -
One by one they left my side,
Talking as they downed home-brewed potcheen,
But I kept watch with constant salutes.

Whisky fumes fought petrol haze
As I looked below to the breaking crests.
I watched as a jellyfish floated past
Like flowering kale, it billowed out.

I slowly felt its lethargy sting -
My arms grew weary and my head floated,
Searching for long-lost territory.
But I tugged, tugged, to the thumps of the engine.

It happened then - I felt a panic -
Stronger and stronger it struggled from me.
I jumped up and down: 'I've got one! I've got one!' but
I caught more then than I could have known.

My great-uncle staggered over, chuckling
He helped me wind in the reel.
The line retracted in his hook-scarred hands -
Under and over, around the handle.

And slowly the prize came up to me,
A silver salver with no first place gold.
Its scales thrashed about, suspended mid-air -
Flailing like anonymous legs at a hanging.

My joy was far from polystyrene blue
And hospital-white bleached shelves,
But all joy died as warm guts were harpooned out
And thrown onto the deck.

Guilt swam through me then.
Flecked with pink, I longed for my mother.

I went to Tesco the week after,
To the mortuary with metal-crushed ice.
Its clammy fillets were cling-filmed -
A cold blanket I could not peel off.

James Heaney

Adrian

Now I have a bin that gets a spin,
same as all the others
and you've gone
and forgotten my name
but once we were bin brothers.

As the machine comes round weekly,
flashing and grinding
I salute and shout:
'Hey up Adrian!' but I get blank looks
for all my comradely reminding.

Do you remember a bin Adrian
do you remember a bin?

And the black art of black bagging
and our belts that were sagging
with gifts for housewives when
we peeled off a new bag or two
and the scurrying trail, house by house

and the humping and the dumping
of fresh piles on the pavements
to be scooped up and tossed
into the yawning back of the trawling
wagon with a button that we pressed
to bring the jaws together to compress
another week's worth;
submit it to landfill.

I'm a punter, on the other side
of the route that still brings in your butter
now but once I was bin cabin crew,
front line, like you, working
the revolving ride.

You were already
in the midst of your marathon then
- binning as you had been since the beginning -
now you're all high-vis it's a new garb-
age and they've reinvented the wheel,

I look out behind the grey and green
barrel-chested parade
where I stand concealed.

You can't root in the rubbish anymore
the back of your mind is clean
from all that rise and shine
and cymbal crashing
as you march with the machine.

Daniel Greenwood

Summer With A Toddler

Summers used to be a time
when I'd relax and laze around,
play some music in the garden,
and listen as I browned.

It was the height of relaxation
with the birds up in the trees,
the butterflies flitting about
and the buzzing of the bees.

Well that's all gone to pot
now I have a child in tow,
I don't have time to relax
as he's always on the go.

He runs up to the butterflies,
excited when they land,
he calls me over to see
then tries to squash them with his hand.

We point out all the birds
he likes to do it every day,
but the birds are all called Bob
as it's easier for him to say.

His favourite 'toy' outside
is our brand new garden hose,
he likes to water *everything*
including all his clothes.

I'd try to sit down for a rest
and watch him playing in the sand,
but I'd barely warm the seat
before he'd grab me by the hand.

Up! Up! Up! He'd cry excitedly
for me to follow, as off he races,
I'd have to join him in the sandpit
(getting sand lodged in some places).

He certainly keeps me fit
tearing around and having fun,
as I chase him with the suncream
to protect him from the sun.

So my time is now spent running around
and pushing him in his swing,
my lazy days are officially over...
but I wouldn't change a thing!

Nicola Gooch

Two Photographs

How many of them?
Hundreds I suppose,
All looking up at
The camera above.

Most wearing flat caps,
Some wearing boaters,
A few wearing bowlers,
Just ordinary blokes.

The caption says,
The young men of August,
British recruits waiting
For their pay.

Another photograph almost the same
Of men wearing boaters,
A few wearing bowlers,
Yet not so many wearing flat caps.

The caption says,
In Berlin, a German officer
Reads out the Kaiser's orders.

Two photographs dated August 1914,
Almost the same, one taken in London
One in Berlin.

I suppose it was not long
Before they were wearing helmets of steel
And uniforms of different designs.

And that they did what they had never
Thought that they would ever do
Nor ever dreamt it.

And in the years that followed,
Those that survived that martyrdom
Saw their wasted sacrifice
Some twenty years on.

I cannot help but feel sad
Looking at two photographs
Knowing with hindsight that for
Some of them violent death came.

It is their innocence
Of what was coming
That touches me the most.

Robert W Lockett

Rootage

Precariously poised. This style,
from country lane, bestows
sweet sense of summer as she
soaks up water meadows.

Gangling grasses flush with flowers,
wild and fancy free,
flourish as the river, now
in bed, flows out to sea.

Peek-a-boo! An otter breach!
A plop, then playful peep!
Stately swans move currently
en route to nests in reeds.

A flash of orange, hint of blue,
king of fishers air-streams through.
Ducks and coots dip in and out;
pert bottoms pointing skyward.

On the brink of ancient weirs
a pedestal for Pisces prey:
posing heron's planned upkeep,
preparation under way.

Spanning over streaming flow,
where Canford boathouse lays,
an auld suspension footbridge
harping to Victorian days.

Moving depths conceal much.
Externals cause a breach from line.
Water needs a leveller;
as does humankind.

Change of mind calls temptingly.
Quintessential town could wait.
Skirt market and the Minster:
upstream connect. And
(I become contented bait!)

Timbered hill, removed to right,
encloses tracks and paths...
... linking old New Forest
to this pastoral place.

Beryl Jupp

Knot Eye

He farmed, she watched the shop, they played, he talked.
Here was a community with apple trees and silken grass,
a book group gathering each month, the boys on bikes,
the church room's group, the village fete and
dogs unleashed,
sorrow when a gardener lost her path and Dennis lost
his sheep.
The apples dropped, there was a wedding in the church;
old ladies died and weeds, like ordnances, bloomed once, then
went to harass other boroughs, other village seams.
The castle held its roster of events, the river flowed beneath.
This was a world, you'd think, where all adhered
and order was observed and none complained.

Then came Attenborough, George Monbiot and Gaia James;
We'll be frying in the heat, we're killing Earth, we have
to change!
What! Give up my lovely kitchen range, my 4X4, my
golden ink?
You think I want to dwell on such rare and distant things?
And change my life, the way I vote and dress and what
I buy?

Oh I, oh me? Not eye! You think my eye is knotted shut,
I can't see what it is I need to know, I'm in a blinkered rut?
Oh tut, not I. I cook, I sew, I feel, I read, I listen to the radio
and take in all the news. You think I'm gullible? I believe
in common ratios and what the status quo believe; isn't
that enough?

You say we'll burn? Not eye. I clearly see the way to go
with Attenborough so long as he remains remote on my TV
and doesn't smite my conscience when I sleep.

A vision purled with skeins of diffidence, indifference, denial?
Our eyes are knotted shut by time and pace and
clotted views?
We're no longer animals who move so calm and wild
and free?
But I'm in charge; I control the knots, the carbon paths
that lead
to my supremacy; I clearly see what I am meant to do
as long as it enhances me, my life, the core of who I am
and why,
of all the earth's components, I am entitled to my
elevated place.

I would axe the final old-growth redwood tree, net the last
remaining cod, pour diminished ancient sunlight in
my Jaguar;
I would press the entire earth down on its knees to ensure this
space
would satisfy my every want. I will not suffer scarcity, not eye! Not
yet.
Now, to the village fete, the laughter and the pint;
Go on, place your bets. I am a clever ape. I will survive.

Karen Eberhardt-Shelton

Metamorphosis

You told me you loved me

you lied...

for just as a sculptor
works on his latest creation
you transformed me
from the person
you vowed to honour and cherish.

Using belittlement and humiliation
as mallet and chisel
you painstakingly chipped away
my confidence and self-esteem
until all that stood,
was the outline of an effigy
permeated with
self-doubt and self-loathing

then

utilising disparagement as your emery
you diligently sanded down
any remaining shards of my self-respect
to complete your masterpiece

the subjugated me

for years,
servitude and acquiescence
was all I knew
until the day love found me
encased in your contemptuous cocoon

real love,

love that gave the strength
and courage I needed
to affect a metamorphosis;

breaking free from my penal pupa
I spread my new wings

and flew away.

Janette Fisher

Holocaust

60 years ago today six million souls led away to die
No one could hear them plead or cry
Their only crime was to be of different creed
Disabled, outcasts, infirm, homosexuals, or from a so-called
different breed
Not only one race, but any person with an outsider's face
All who didn't meet the needs of a purified so-called
master race
Those that didn't fit in to a master plan
The ideals of a bullying, lying, cheating, scheming
Austrian man
He led those to believe they were off to a new way of life
Taking those out of poverty and inner-city strife
To a new camp of luxury where they would 'work to be free'
And above the camps' entrances the deceiving signs 'Arbeit macht
frei'
All those hoarded from all over Europe into
unknown elimination
Fooled, misled, as they sang and were full of celebration
But little did they know the fate
That behind the mask of those who tricked them was a race of
pure hate
And as the air rained white ash and the furnaces burned white hot
Were those millions at that time, to be burned and lost forever
and forgot
That arrogant man who thought he could win the world
Through greed and ignorance watched his plans fall apart,
become unfurled
Panic as he lost his grip of tyranny and fear and lost the war
To hide the biggest secret of all
But as most things it came to light

The world now heard the voice of those victims' plight
Something the human race should never allow to
happen again
And there to this very day stands the epitaphs of
those remains
Those concentration camps there to remind us of this all
As those six millions voices call

Not one tear shed
Not one voice heard
Not one plea accepted
Not one soul forgotten
Not one life wasted
Not one death
Not one lost heart
Not one belief
Not one individual
But one of six million all as one
Now my remembrance is done

Terry J Powell

Deep

The rain lashed down
Fast and angry
Drenching you to the bone
As you stand bare
Whilst your tears
Mingle with the rain
Dance and rave
In fury and fire
Burning deep within
Your body
Shivers and quakes
In temper and rage
Rain and tears
Stream like a torrid river
Flowing faster
Picking up speed
Then crashing
Like broken glass
Upon the ground
Tiny pieces shattering
As you tumble
Naked and alone
Beneath the flood
Swirling into blackness
Despair and frustration
Disappearing out of control
Heavier and heavier
The rain falls
As you try to stand
Push back against
The flowing waterfall

Holding you deep
In the darkest well
Fighting to find
The spark of light
Some hope to cling to
Drying the tears
And finally
Stop feeling
So naked and alone.

Gail Underwood

The Girl In The Field

Once in a field there was a girl,
Who would manipulate everything around her,
The flowers that grew there,
The green grass,
The bugs,
The worms,
The earth beneath her feet,

Her manipulation was so great she would sing to the flowers for
them to bend her way,
But when they could bend no more,
They died and withered away.

The grass she touched was green,
But before long it would dry up,
Blacken and die,
Leaving patches in the ground,

She played with the bugs,
Crushing them under her weight,

The worms she bribed from the earth with scandalous ease,
To devour them at her need and whim,

Soon everything around her was gone,
No matter how she tried,
No matter how much she destroyed around her,
She couldn't see,
The girl in the field was cold,

But no matter how much blood she spilled in desperation,
The lies she spoke to it,
Or how she tried to beg,
Clutching at dead straw,
The earth would never take her,

No peace, just pain,

The girl in the field,
Who now weeps,
Because she has reaped the evil she did sow.

Lauren Cullen

The Starlight

Sparkling tears on a dark velvet sky
Witnessing moon and nights walking by
Just raise a hand and feel their spikes
Lifeless beauties enchanting my eyes.

We love them, we dress them with romance and hopes
Our deepest desires embrace their corpse.
We seek them, caress them, hoping one day
We'll be as amazing and great as are they.

Our God and ancestors are walking their ways
We raise our eyes, we send our praise,
Our hearts, our minds cannot compromise
With thoughts that such beauties do not bear life.

I'm asking my angel to send me a ray
A spike from a star to lighten my way.
My angel did hear my prayer and despair
He's sending the light I thought I desire.

And day after day I'm loving the light
My heart full of joy, my soul in disguise.
The light is as cold as the star in the sky
Gets warmth from my veins to go on and survive.

And then one good day the light understands:
It's taking my life, but I don't make demands
I'm giving it all: warmth, life, mind and goal
I'm dying each day, the light feeds from my soul.

Who is to blame? The light? Me? The life?
The body that cries for love and for lies?
The soul which is trapped and amazed by the mind?
The heart which refuses to see and is blind?

The light feels alive, enjoying my warmth,
It plays with life, with small joys and my heart,
But knows that one day it will go along
Rejoining the star where all lights belong.

Anna Grace

When I Grow Up

When I was younger I wanted to fly,
To get on a rocket and see the stars fly by.
Travel the universe and be home for tea,
Well that was my job when I was three.

Then you start school and have to be serious,
Well they can't make me, they must be delirious.
I was about fun and wanted to be an inventor,
But it turns out at eight I wasn't a good experimenter.

By eleven I wanted to be a sprinter,
Training all year, even through winter.
Even though I was fast, I couldn't keep up,
So my job as a sprinter was given up.

At thirteen I wanted to be a zookeeper,
To look after all animals, but never be a beekeeper.
Penguins and monkeys would be a dream to work with,
But at thirteen that job was definitely a myth.

Then at fifteen I sprang out the box,
A job chasing tornados, left my parents in a flummox.
For the beauty in raw nature was it for me,
But perhaps I should just stick to watching them on TV.

Now I'm nineteen and thought I had grown,
But there's a whole world out there, so many skills to hone.
People keep asking what I want my job to be,
Well maybe I should just tell them to 'wait and see'.

Don't they see the opportunities out there to grab?
Perhaps I'll try science and end up in a lab.
Or maybe a designer with my own fashion line,
Or buy a vineyard and make fine wines.
I'm not certain anymore what my job will be,
But perhaps nineteen will be the year I learn to ski.

Portia-Hope Kitney

Shysters

Thou art and ever more shall be -
Chancers, weathercocks and trimmers;
The acrobats and hatchet-men
Of any denomination;
Defalcators who come at you
With stiletto smiles and scatter
Contagion like consumptives' spittle,
Their victims blackened by buboes.

All well-known predators, scavengers
With hooked beaks and taste for carrion,
Their demon wings spreading shadows
Of death and abomination;
They jostle and hiss and squeal,
Fighting over the cadaver
Until its well-picked bones revealed
Lie white as sepulchres on the sand.

Tyranny each deity knows
As absolute certainty;
Fashioned by sakers and culverins,
The tapestries are all burning
In homes sacked and sucked out like eggs,
While soldiers scurry in haste
Loading the bodies onto carts
Somewhere to decay seamlessly.

Whoremongers, rabble and scum,
Unerring in infamy;
The dross always rises like flotsam,
Choking the kindly and good,
Leaving the children's toys broken,
The pure linen soiled and sodden
With urine: I do not know
If they shall ever see God.

John Hutcheson

Olivia In Twinkleland

Every night in Twinkleland,
Olivia wished upon a star!

One day the Crooked Crone planned...
To steal each and every star!

On her icky mucky stick,
She flew high up in the sky.

The crone played her nasty trick,
And plucked all stars in one try!

The crone stuck them to her dress,
It looked pretty for the dance.

So Olivia was in distress,
And wanted to take a chance.

She summoned the Twinkle fairy,
Who sprinkled all twinkly sparkle!

She swapped all the stars stud glary,
With pure diamonds that did twinkle!

The crone was stirring her brew,
With her head inside her pot.

So never found what was true...
Of her blue dress on the cot!

Then the crone danced in the rain,
And the fairy flew afar!

And then every night again,
Olivia wished upon a star!

Kavita Kulkarni Frary

Mr B

The choir sang in hearty voices,
All in tune, except a boy at the back
(Opening his lungs with the greatest of vigour)
Was decidedly... no, maybe not... yes... decidedly flat.

Mr B sighed, but soon rallied round,
(Remembering the chaos when he'd arrived),
The choir mistress had tried her very hardest,
But minus piano player, the choir had barely survived.

Now, she clapped her hands with glee,
'They're so much better,' she gushed with delight,
'Except for the boy who sings flat at the back,
They've completed a song, with the words nearly right!'

Mr B smiled and joined in the applause,
Felt proud for the children who had given their all,
Glad he'd helped them on their long journey,
And cheered as they took their next curtain call.

Then one day, retired, and strolling somewhere,
Shopping for Christmas, wasting money on tat,
Mr B heard singing - lusty, joyous singing,
But decidedly... no, maybe not... yes... decidedly flat.

'Hello, Mr B!' the singer said heartily,
(Giving Mr B's hand an almighty slap),
'Thanks to the help you gave me in school,
I'm a singer now, quite successful - and I can even rap!'

The motto of this story is - never make predictions
Of what path someone's life will take in the future,
It needs more than just the voice to gain you fame
and fortune -
Success nowadays is all about character.

C A Mackie

It

(A love poem for the romantically uninclined.)

There was never any controlling it
No dodging it. Unloading it
It sealed us both together and held us tightly in its grip.
We tried our hand at moulding it
Healing it and holding it
It wanted us together; head, heart and even hip

Once, we nearly cornered it
We threatened it. We warned it
But it came once more and sheltered us, till we fought with it
again.
Black, bruised, we gently eased it
We blew on it and teased it
We rescued and revived it, till it burst back into flame

Life drove us and we dashed it
We trashed it. We thrashed it
Tested every fibre, every ounce of strength it had.
We badgered it and blagged it
My God! How we have shagged it!
Reignited, it then gave us, all the pleasure that it had

Without pause we have abused it.
Never soothed it. Smoothed it
Caressed or contemplated, its very gentle deeds.
We hounded it. Confounded it
In drink, we damn near drowned it!
But still it softened life for us and satisfied our needs

So, this 'It', it lays between us
Beautifully binding us. Bleeding us
The tether and the freedom that only it can give
Still searing us. Endearing us
Together, there is no fear in us
This It we share between us, is the reason that we live.

Kim Greenacre

The Curse Of
Mental Health

When your heart is full
Of anger and doubt
And you can't think of a way
To let it all out

When you're doing your best
Not to lose control
But disorder and chaos
Consume your soul

When you try to make it better
But it ends up worse
And you get struck down
By this evil curse

When your armour wears thin
And you can't fight back
There's a war in your mind
It's a brutal attack

When you can't make sense
Of what's truth and what's lies
And the tears start building
And burning your eyes

When you look into the mirror
And despise your reflection
You see that it's you
But can't make the connection

When you're struck by the curse
Of mental health
Your cruellest enemy
Becomes yourself.

Jade Bradley-Melling

The Forgotten Kitten

Mummy cat was feeling fine, washing all her kittens nine
But, hello, what is all this? Something here is quite amiss
For one small furry mite is not exactly right.
He's smaller than the other eight, poor mummy cat is in
a state.
'What shall I do?' she cries in woe. 'One kitten bad and I
feel low.'

The other kittens didn't mind, that's not to say they
were unkind
They had all that they could wish for and did not want or need
one more
Poor little kitten small and weak he had no strength his food to
seek
So when it was time for all to lunch the others rushed forward in a
bunch
Not caring that one small wee cat was left behind upon
the mat

Forgotten by his family, no breakfast, lunch or even tea!
But wait a minute, who is this here to take away the
kitten's fear?
A little boy has seen his plight and plans to rescue him
from fright
'Look Dad,' he cries, 'oh can't you see that's the pussycat
for me
The other ones are all quite bad for making him so very sad!'

So Daddy takes the little lad into the shop for he's
quite glad
That his darling smallest boy wants a pet and not a toy
The shopkeeper takes them to the place where all the cats are in
a case
He waits to see what the lad will choose and thinks he knows
what he'll refuse
But wait a minute, he's chosen that, the smallest, weakest little
cat!

Upon my soul he says to Dad, 'Your little boy must be
quite mad!'
His father did not really mind because at heart he was
quite kind
And secretly believed that all should have their chance both big
and small
So now there's no denying that our puss is quite the
master cat
For he has caught up in height and weight since now all is his
that's on his plate.

Royston E Herbert

Once Upon A Time

It was cold night in December
The moon was shining bright.
Patsy Brown often went walking
Yes even at this time of night.
She loved to hear the night sounds,
They were haunting but gave her no fright.
She had done this for many years
Yes even at this time of night.
She sat on an old tree that had fallen
Blown down it had been a fearsome sight.
She had sat there many times with her father
Yes even at this time of night.
Suddenly out of the bushes a man swept
She could see he was all in the nude.
She looked up and down his body
She thought what she saw was rather rude.
She called, 'What do you think you are doing
Running like that wearing not even a stitch?'
The man looked embarrassed and cold
He looked down and his body gave a little twitch.
'I am sorry but someone stole them
I am camping out here in the wood.
I was fast asleep when they took them
I would cover myself if I could.'
Patsy took off her coat from around her
She handed it to him this man that was turning blue.
He took the coat from her, though rather too small
But he told her that it would do.

A voice came out of the darkness
The voice was calling her name
'Wake up!' the voice was calling
Her dreams have never since been the same.

Barry Scott Crisp

Adjusting

I saw him in the sunless room;
I saw him: old, hunched,
puckered as a slept-on
pillow. His spidery arms smoothed
down his thinning hair,
cuckoo spit-coloured; tangled
like a broken cobweb.

He rose at dawn,
whistled his sailor whistle,
sought out his imaginary cord:
twin tendrils from heaven; his rigging
to free him from his slumber.

I saw him light the fire.
I saw him through the fuzz,
wiping sleep from my eyes.
He rekindled the coals:
an indoor campfire where stories are told:
tales of the Wiltshire giant
who lit cigarettes from the gas light.
My saucer eyes lit wide with awe,
waiting... always waiting,
wanting to hear more.

I saw him as night drew in,
I saw him ready to shut out the light.

Dead on five, the smell of ash
hung in the air. He pulled shut each blind:
the blackout camouflaged his home,
keeping out the sunless night. Then, I saw him
switch off my indoor sun.

Jacquie Williams

War

The battle of the Somme
Husbands, brothers, sons
Never to come home
Lost to the enemy guns
Over the top they were sent
With courage, fear and fright
No questions, they just went
They knew they had to fight
In thousands they did fall
But forever they will live
In hearts and minds of all
Who respect what they did give
They did it for their king
And loved ones left behind
Oh, the ballads they did sing
To take war off their mind
One hundred years now passed
A generation lost
From a war not meant to last
Was it really worth the cost
Remembrance, respect and pride
We never will forget
Our tears we'll never hide
For men we never met
Their names live on in stone
Their bodies no one knows
They'll never be alone
In fields where the poppy grows
War is harsh, loss is high

So never forget the price
The cost those brave men paid to die
Is the ultimate sacrifice.

Amanda Crowden

Survived The Winter

The threat of ice, the threat of snow,
Made it a place I didn't want to go.

To feel the sharpness of a wind so cruel,
Like many before them, the seasons duel.

The tall tree stands so silent and strong,
In the middle of nowhere is where it belongs.

Through the beating of ice, the harshness of hail,
Is what makes it such a wonderful tale.

It fought off winter and survived till Spring,
The tree is just the bravest thing.

The roots embedded in the soil so deep,
Is just like the soul with secrets to keep.

Engraved are initials that have dented the bark,
Mirroring the scars I have on my heart.

Shaking her blossoms, they fall like rain,
Making it possible to grow once again.

Underestimating the struggle the winter affirmed,
Gave true self-belief and a lesson well learned.

This tree grows faith, conviction and hope,
Showing us all that we can cope.

Doesn't matter what season - the tree did not fall,
You survived the winter; you can survive them all.

Tracey Robertson

Red Alert

'More floods in the north,' says the man on TV,
They've issued another red alert.
More sandbags to stack across more front doors,
Desperate to hold back nature's power.

They've issued another red alert.
A few hours warning is all they can give.
Desperate to hold back nature's power;
Remembering how it was last time.

A few hours warning was all they could give;
A chance to move what they can upstairs.
Remembering how it was last time;
Knowing just what lies ahead.

A chance to move what they can upstairs,
As they nervously wait for the ominous sound.
Knowing just what lies ahead,
When the waters surge through the narrow street.

As they nervously wait for the ominous sound,
They do what they can to limit the heartache,
When the waters surge through the narrow street.
They offer a prayer to whoever will hear.

They do what they can to limit the heartache.
More sandbags to stack across more front doors.
They offer a prayer to whoever will hear.
'More floods in the north,' says the man on TV.

Bryn Strudwick

Moscow Winter

Imagine a city in winter,
Buildings reaching for the sky
And the ice will slowly splinter;
Weather so cold, it could make you cry.
The square is made from black-cobbled stones,
Crowds everywhere you look.
The chilled sting will numb your bones
Exactly like out of a book.
Yet the white wanderers whisper
Amongst the crowds.
They make the air crisper
As they advance from the clouds.
Those dancers perform
A flurry of pirouettes,
Create a colourless storm
Leaving only silhouettes.
Through the gale of tiny
Ghosts you can spot
The nine domes, always shiny
And so dearly bought.
The colours are so radiant,
Yet fascinatingly ancient.

Tsar Ivan the Terrible
Found it unbearable
To look upon anything more divine
So he removed his eyes
Thinking he was wise
Because he would not see it decline.

Anastasia Maciver

Walking On

Dusk, the end of a long day
Light fading fast,
I stand and listen
Taking in the sounds of nature around me.

Crows are cawing raucously
As they come in to roost
In a nearby copse,
And a blackbird sings its goodbye to the day.

The hoot of an early owl
Carries on the still evening air,
As I stand and reflect on the day,
I remember the early start across dew-clad fields.

The ploughman's lunch and good honest pint
I had enjoyed at a pub along the way,
The view as I crossed the moor
The feeling of sun on my back.

A breeze sprang up from nowhere,
Rustling leaves, disturbing crows,
And rippling the grass in the meadow
Like waves on the seashore.

Bringing a perfect day to a close
And leaving me to wonder,
As I head for the coast.
What will tomorrow bring?

Kenneth Capps

Anger

When she first saw her, after it happened,
Still, pale and simply gone, along with her unborn son
She felt a kaleidoscope of emotion.

Anger: How could her sister do this, leave her -
without a sibling, to do the best for her only niece,
To be alone in the end, to lose yet another nephew.

Alone: To care for her parents, without aid
As age stalked them, when they needed support
A survivor to live on, now forever sibling-less.

Pity: For all her sister had been through
And must have gone through in her last moments
having to leave her life and precious daughter.

Sadness: Because of the loss of her sibling's booming laugh
Her love, loyalty and their shared story
The laughs and tears, their memories.

Guilt: She was the older, why her little sister
Who never saw 33, she survived, why? For how long
She may live to be old, but not her sister, the
unfairness, why?

Grief: At the chaos that then unfolded
Her raw emotions, her parents' double loss

For her six-year-old niece who was to grow up motherless.

Charlotte Trevor

The Reward Of Waiting In The West Coast Of Scotland

Blue sky pushes cloud eastwards
Light grey now at six o'clock of the evening
After day's rain and mountain mist.
Heavy cloud lingers to enfold
The islands of Skye and Rhum and Egge
Whilst nearer Muck basks its full length
In end of day's repose.

Sanna's light green and gold
Encircle the bay landwards
Viewed across bright bell heather clumps,
Pale wedgewood-blue and delicate harebell,
And white anemone cups which hold up their
scalloped heads
To welcome the evening sun.

Little waves run and chase and jump high in competition
Over the shallow rocks out to sea.
Near at hand the energetic, lively, purposeful
Tide-coming - in waves
Delight our ears and eyes.
The sea deepens to blue-grey at last.

Oystercatcher's shrill piccolo cry
Flies across the ivory piano keys of the sea,
Running up and down the scale *allegro scherzando*
Orchestrated now by the sun's majestic rays.
The finale has begun and rises to a joyful conclusion
After one day's long waiting.

Margaret Holden

Old Parlour Tricks Of The Fallen Angel

Old parlour tricks of the fallen angel
Drop of whisky for the eyes to make them dazzle
A little streak of mercury to thicken her lashes
Concoction of chemicals in which she washes
On the table, tin basin, half full of water
Reduced to live in such ruthless squalor
Arsenic for the skin, to whiten like porcelain
Down the hatch with a sip of laudanum

Old parlour tricks of the fallen angel
To ease the pain she makes herself beautiful
To be desired, to make her living
In the hands of men, so unforgiving
Madam rules and takes her cut
Egg timer turned, count the seconds, *tick-tock*
No time to waste, she succumbs to the client
Till the sands run out, she must be compliant

Old parlour tricks of the fallen angel
No way to tell, the hidden danger
She has a bell which she can ring
In times of endangerment or overpowering
In a tiny booth, she works deep underground
Secret tunnels for men, sinful deeds to be found
Old parlour tricks of the fallen angel
Living on the edge of society's moral favour.

Nicola Graham

A Mind Like Mine

At the end of every day
every mistake
that I make
and stupid word I say
will start to replay.
And it's hard to unwind
or leave it all behind
with the day on rewind
inside a mind like mine.

When you know what to do,
'cause they keep telling you
what you know to be true:
you've done all you can do,
it's still not easy to forget
those stupid things that I said.
Peace can be so hard to find
with a mind like mine.

And you have those worksheets
in your bag for days like these
that you're supposed to work through
to get your thinking somewhere new,
but the thought of digging deep
gives you shed loads of unease -
you're so scared of what you'll find
when you've got a mind like mine.

And those are the days I need
you to find my missing peace,
or even missing pieces
of this jigsaw incomplete.
And that's when I know
I'm asking for more than you can show
because it might be untold
but it's there, underlined, in bold!

I wish that I could say
all of this to you today
and somehow make you understand
what it feels like in 'my land',
or what it means when you're so kind
to this silly mind of mine
when I barely deserve the patience,
never mind the time.

So I hope you can forgive me
I'm getting better, slowly,
a work in progress
a current mess,
but with a little time
I know I'll be alright
if I keep fighting the good fight;
keeping all thoughts set
on God above
inside this mind of mine.

And while you wait, just know my healing
is something I'm receiving
from a God that gives me all I need
to live beyond my feelings.
He is my refuge, my fortress,
and shelter from all distress
can be found within His arms
when heavy thoughts begin to oppress.

I trust the One who lifts my head up,
run the race, and never give up,
so thankful for His loving kindness,
keep on praising through the sadness.
He is the One thing
I require,
the One thing I desire
and nothing
nothing
can separate me
from His perfect love;
no depth, no height
that you can find,
never mind a mind like mine.

Frankie Wilkinson

To You, Orb Weaver

Enlaced in her ambivalence,
with presence that would mesmerise.
Such locks of russet embers lay reflected in oceanic eyes.
She'd speak a song inquisitive,
yet every note relieving,
Still I know of every pinnacle
that surely she's concealing.
A might of dignified content
would mask regret of forlorn days,
When searching for a reason,
would that reason lay disdained?
That voice resounds through
such memory in your array,
Spoken sweet through cautious lips,
a masquerade display.
Each shade, an affectation...
So piercing is your effervescence,
woven through in silken rays.
Her lustre shaded in angelic sight,
displacing me with every gaze.
Incarcerated by your thoughts,
to dream of liberated days,

Your imagery in hourglass,
reminding me my time with you decays...

Steven Kuhn

Take Us Somewhere, Driver

Take us somewhere driver, take us away from this
dreary strip.
We drive on through the hissing sodium lights,
He plays Arabic music too loud and we laugh in
spasmodic declension.
I can't hear what you are saying -
We're here, get out.
Between the gas works and the shunting yard the big top squats
on the potato fields,
The giant tent hovers over the red clay like your nanny's skirts,
weighed down by the oppressive heat.
Jerome is casing my face, and making unnecessary altruistic
confessions for the benefit of no one, for the titillation of
a girl.
The bearded lady rattles her can - shake, shake.
As we near the boiling throng I feel a tap on my shoulder,
Let go of me.
The waxwork ghost grabs my wrist, nails as sharp as her hair is
dark.
I have no money for you old woman,
The nails dig deeper,
Let me read it please.
There was a moment's pause - a theatrical sigh,
She looks up and says;
You will make money and your children will all have strong white
teeth -
A laugh that could get you burned as a witch.
The gnarled finger points to my feline companion,
She is not the one.

Yellow pupils flash in the dark, my young friend giggles nervously. You will never be happy, she is already gone, her pretty face bloated and blue, smiles at the catfish in the bottom of the bayou.

Matt Martin

Equations

One plus one is two,
Two plus two is four,
The more you love yourself
The more we love you, sure.

Three plus three is six,
Six plus six is twelve,
The more you love your mix,
The more you love yourselves.

Ten, twenty, thirty, forty,
Count your strengths both nice and naughty.
Fifty, sixty, seventy, eighty,
Flaws and flairs are all weighty!

They could be hundreds,
They could be zero,
As embracing them makes you a hero!
Add, minus, multiply, divide -
What are those things which you so hide?

Length, breadth, width and height,
Self-love is your dear might!
It could be a sum; it could be an equation,
But loving yourself does breed love in the nation!

Sudakshina Bhattacharjee

Feathers

The crow watches the day
The owl watches the night
What they see neither can say
Whether wrong or right

The dark raven owns us all
With wings of coal-black
Listen for its bleak call
And never look back.

Smile at the dove
The heavenly song it sings
Look for the love
And the peace it brings

Listen to the bleak warning
From each new day dawning
This is the stark new age
With terror taking centre stage

And as we take to flight
A new army uses might
The crow owns the day
The owl controls the night
As we pray to be alright.

Teresa Whaley

The Bus Driver

I like to spend my evenings reading whisky,
Sipping a short story:

'There's shampoo in our protagonist's eyes. He squeezes them
tighter. It starts stinging'.
Just
Give
In.

The character continues to aggravate me.
'I've wanted to drive buses since four years old; to be the best bus
driver in the county'
The ice in my tumbler tears, I wash away the vexation. Vapours
soothe my lungs.

I gasp.

At four years old I achieved as an astronaut.
As the omnipotent creator of a playtime paradise:

A Lego fire station, snipped up straws for hoses, vehicles from
other toy worlds,
worlds carved out of Plasticine.
People portrayed through action figures that lost their clothes.
Crayon murals of mummy and daddy plastering the kitchen walls;
magnetic letters
Painting poetry on every radiator. Rabbi to all the teddy bears'
weddings.

I flick through faster,
A sip, a shiver.
A bus driver,
Since the age of four.

R P Thomas

Just Like You

If you strip off my age, gender, nationality
Race, religion, sexuality
I am a mere human being
Just like you.

I have not personally harmed you
Nor caused any crippling affliction
So do not stand here making it sound as if
Violence is my addiction.

Different religions believe in different holy books
But within those religions people interpret with
different outlooks
So to say you and I belong in the same religion, our understanding
must be identical
Is a great generalisation in itself inherently wrong.

Each human being must be treated as an individual
Not in the shadow of another vile person
To say he did this and so they all must be like that
Is an assumption provoking rumours and unnecessary hurt.

Strip off and see
You are a human being just like me
That reason is good enough
For why we should exist in equality.

Nishita Choudhury

A Day At The Coast

The soft sand glistens brightly
In the warm and shining sun
You can hear the seagulls in the air
And children having fun
The sea does spray you mildly
As the waves do gently roam
The saltiness it fills the air
And the water starts to foam
As dinner time approaches
Most people's favourite dish
Is served up on the sea front
The lovely fresh cooked fish
An hour in the arcade
And then for my next stop
A nice big ice cream from the van
Then move on to the shop
So much rock and candy
And little souvenirs
Bookmarks, keyrings, magnets too
And postcards of the piers
Time to head for home now
As the sun is going down
With all my fun fond memories
Of this little seaside town.

Moira Newton

Our Gran's Soup

Our gran used to make us soup,
A steaming golden broth.
It stood out like a work of art,
Against the pearl-white table cloth.

Full of barley, peas and lentils
And leek of emerald-green,
It was the most mouth-watering soup
That I had ever seen.

So expectantly, we all sat
Around the dining table.
Eagerly waiting for our soup,
As Gran wielded the ladle.

Into the giant soup pan,
She dipped the mighty spoon.
We sat there reverentially,
It couldn't come too soon.

Finally all our bowls were filled,
And Gran said, 'Carry on.'
And to the sound of happy slurping,
The soup was quickly gone.

Gary Smith

Poets Anonymous

Hello,
My name is John Doe and I'm a poet.
It's been twenty-four hours since I wrote my last one.
It was supposed to be in iambic pentameter,
But it came out in a rash of caesurae and enjambments,
So it scanned like Shakespeare on speed.
I'm trying to do it right, but it's hard, you know?
Some days I just have to scribble some doggerel,
Or even Christmas card rhymes just to get my fix.
Other days, the alliteration just pours promptly from my pen,
Or the stanzas simply scroll across my screen.
Those days though, those delicious days, are few;
Even then, the idyllic, dactylic rhyme can seem imbecilic
If it doesn't flow fluently on the page.
I'm sorry for all those I've assaulted with dissonant assonance,
Or the hubris of hyperspatial hyperbole.
I will try to make amends,
Without overtaxing the syntax.
I'm taking it just one day at a time;
A few couplets, a quatrain or two.
Maybe on the good days some faltering free verse,
Or a voluptuous villanelle.
I can do it.
I know I can.

Trevor Alexander

Poem Snapshots Of My Town In The Heatwave

My forebears left their footprint on the sands,
The sea, charged with tender gentleness
Of all those who found their last sleep in her embrace
Laps upon the sands and sings of man's eternity.

Now, reflected on the rippling waves,
The dipping sunbeams, glinting on the sand,
Spread eastwards to the darkening shore,
And lights come on, like neon necklaces,
Along Great Yarmouth's Golden Mile,
Past the horse-drawn landaus,
Past the jean-clad legs and teensy T-shirts
Of giggling, arm-clasping girls,
And, following behind, a leather-jacketed gang
Of man-hooded, pleasure-seeking lads.
Yet they too are harassed.
For their time is curbed by parking metres,
Cold time-keepers, like eagle-eyed janitors,
Along the kerbside, silent and malevolent,
Whose presence must be heeded.
Lest the thrill-seeking, little-lasting evening,
Be cruelly crushed and curtailed - at crippling cost.

But earlier, in the pleasure gardens,
Beneath the cool green canopy of trees
Summer-loving couples kiss and forget;
Forget the frazzled faces that flock past
The candyfloss stalls and burger bars

Away towards the sea - wide golden beach
Where children play on pebbled shore,
But here, here in the lush leafy park
Sun-scorched, there is a certain silence
As if the town pauses to take breath
And, above the age-old trees, the searching sun
Seeks to subjugate all, as though its rays
Might devour all, even those in the park.

The scorching sun in an azure sky
Scalds the shore where lie two skulls,
Sea-smoothed and saddened,
One grimaces, one grins,
Both are void of life
But there exists complicity between them.
It lurks amidst the sand and stones,
While they look on,
The one scowling, the other smiling,
For the sea has swooshed away
Most of their inner selves
Save a slight residue that remains,
Clinging like bladderwrack to sea-lapped rocks.

Now, as summer's lease ends
On cleaving, soaring wings, scything swiftly
Through the scudding cloud, glides the graceful bird
And forsakes the sea-lapped, pebble-strewn shore
And wave-dashed dunes of sand and rippled green grass.
There frisks the wind, torment of yesterday,
Whipping the foam-flecked waves into fury,
Ruffling the papers clasped in the fingers
Of summer sunbathers seeking slumber,

But the wind has ceased its frenzied clamour
And now takes rest on seafront swing hammocks
To await the sun and the graceful bird
That will return when springtime walks the shore
And sunlight gilds the sands again.

Caroline Buddery

A Spent Cartridge

Ryan lies looking at the stars
When the mist lifts, only
Restricted by a Velux window.
Its frames make bars to trees
And houses all around,
Interrupting outside energies.

He can watch the stars
And even see the moon
When the clouds withdraw
And the curtains part
To a view of many heavens:
Patterns, lights as on a runway
To lift-off, escape from close to far.

With them he moves anywhere
But for the soles of his feet
On a mattress in his room.
Yet see: he can beat gravity
And storm a way through space
Eternally, his weight irrelevant
Or so it seems, amounting to nothing
But a spent cartridge!

Diane Burrow

Counting Tigers Instead Of Sheep

I fell out with sleep a while ago and now my old friend never
seems to hang around long,
But it gives me more time for my mind to wander and ponder my
rights and wrongs.
Where I found regrets; I found wisdom and along with tears grew
great strength,
Harsh lessons held a presence, but for the price of
accomplishments from great lengths.
I recall the snaps of my temper and realise my patience is wearing
thin as I grow older,
Alas, too cold at times I shivered; as I remember the ice of my own
cold shoulder.
And when the fire of anger burnt red in my eyes,
I had hoped it was only ever with those I despise,
But I've been hot-headed with those who've held me closest in the
cold,
With a heavy heart of guilt I vow to make amends for the venom
I've told.

I've been lost and upon finding my way, found myself on the right
track but on the wrong train,
Repeating life's lessons until they are learned and with every
failure searching for a positive gain.
I've watched my dreams go up in smoke and felt the burn from
the flames,
But I knew the risk of playing with fire and was prepared to take
the blame,
I wandered down the darkest roads to find the
brightest lights,
Took my greatest risks because I couldn't give up without
a fight.

And through it all I'm fuelled by a stubborn desire
to succeed,
Failure is not an option and I refuse to concede,
Because I know if I ever give in,
It has all been for nothing.

Chelsey Taylor

Boo Jess

On the ocean she does live,
To all in the sea for many years, friends with,
She has a captain on board who wears a parrot on his shoulder,
Gazing through his telescope as the air gets colder.

Coco the parrot squawks as he fluffs up his feathers,
But warm enough, as he's used to all kinds of weathers,
With 50 men for a crew no more and no less,
On this wonderful ship named Boo Jess.

Most are sat dithering, some chattering of teeth,
Thinking about what unknowns lie down beneath,
As one shipmate starts to hum out a tune,
Morale starts to rise as one foretells with runes.

As the sun starts to rise, it warms up the deck,
Ahoy! One of the crew spots an old shipwreck,
The captain, whose name I've not yet told, said,
'Ahoy there mateys! Look sharp and not dead.'

So all the crew jump up with excitement and hope,
The men get prepared by gathering some strong rope,
Ready for orders from their very good captain,
A very loyal crew to him whose name's Fin.

Captain Fin is his name who acquired it from past,
When all he rescued were saved very fast,
He's said to sail through the sea as fast as a shark,
No matter what weather or even in the dark.

He sails Boo Jess who was passed down to him,
From a very well-known captain who was his kin,
When she first set sail she was new to the sea,
Now ten generations have passed, she's 803.

She's very strong and loyal and has never failed,
On all types of ocean, calm or rough seas she's sailed,
And although her timbers creak and her sails very old,
It's as if by magic she stays strong, just like pirates' gold.

Barnacles there's none, and sails are off-white,
She still can be seen in darkest of all nights,
Well on with the rescue of the old shipwreck,
Crew jumps on board of this broken wooden deck.

They search for any crew but apart from all but one,
All is abandoned, broken, not salvageable, all's gone,
The only survivor is a strange little black and white dog,
Who wouldn't leave a small enchanted bit of log.

So all survivors rescued and an enchanted bit of wood,
Is all the Captain Fin can do, on this poor shipwreck he stood,
But just as he is leaving, something green catches his eye,
It is shiny and glistening in the sunlight, no not a greenfly.

A very big emerald in the centre of the ship's wheel,
He plucks it free, examines it very closely, yes it's real,
Back to Boo Jess, gathering up the old ropes,
Captain Fin fixes the emerald on the wheel as a host.

Coco and the little dog play with the enchanted log,
As Captain Fin sails through some mysterious fog,
Boo Jess journeys on looking forward to the next,
How many more can she save before it's time for her to rest?

Micheala Edwards

White Poppies

I hear you
In the quiet down time.
Uninvited, unexpected,
You say, 'Don't be sad...
No good being crazy mad.
No mystery, no misery,
Play Misty, one last time, for me.'
You tried to explain.
A world without your words.
Life will never be the same.
Emotional liberty?
Permission to find happiness,
Rediscover my destiny,
Your voice, infiltrates humdrum days.
Close by, never far away.
Twilight, midnight,
Darkest night, brightest day.
I hear you,
When the bustle of busy life dies down.
In the quiet down time.
Whispers in sterile silver silence,
I hear you, I hear you still, so still.

Amelia Michael

Barcodes In The Sky

She sang songs to the underground, he drew the curtains on
russet mist.
Our long-forgotten ancestors remain concealed, beneath and
beyond dreams.

The universe keeps twinkling, reminds me of your island eyes set
against
isolated winter skies, waiting for the first flush of wild flowers in
spring.

His laughter was wrapped up in a cryptic coffin of stars. Spun out
by the joyful
embrace of a child running into the arms of her mother, weaving
raw human

emotion from silk threads. With the rain came dust in paradise,
magenta sunrise,
saxon blue, subjective high, objective low, free falling with the
horizon every time.

A brave new world of words reimagined, barcodes in the sky,
virtual clouds,
binary realities teetering on six-inch stilettos, glass, air,
augmented shimmering patina.

Trace and measure the darkest of elements against the lightest of
matter.
Relative motion, relative emotion, zero plus minus outside looking
in, inside looking out.

This gravity longs too much, enough to make my heart believe in a soul. Enough to
bring singularity to matter, mass-less symbols fall in the afterglow of dot com events.

Here still busy going nowhere and everywhere in hyper reality as if the earth had met
the sky for the first time. In the stillness of the night summer fades to grey.

Once at one with the rain and the dust in a clandestine world without words, a
world without war, brought up in a gutter universe with glitter shards and worm holes.

Karen Adela Barnes

Abandoned

We all went for a picnic
in the summery wood
they went for a bit of a ramble
and so here I am stood

The picnic sat there soggy
as down came the torrid rain
and grass and plants grew round me
would I see my driver again?

Silver birch now surrounds me
Moss and lichen my new coat
Greenery now my camouflage
home for badgers and stoats

Perhaps in time, they'll find me
and give me some release
in twenty, thirty, forty months
I'll be a museum piece!

Hidden by all this greenery
I need a bit of luck
Now looking after the wildlife
as I wait for the pick-up truck.

Brian Francis Kirkham

An Illegal Oath

It was such a lousy allegation,
Yet it resulted in transportation,
The moment could have remained innocuous
Had the government not made such a fuss -
To sentence them so harshly made no sense,
Though history gives them some recompense.
In the tiny village of Tolpuddle,
Somebody got in a fearful muddle.
The authorities should have let it pass,
The six were supported by working mass,
The authorities never realised
The six should soon become immortalised.
Not really that much of a felony;
Injustice cried, 'The penal colony!'
So a prison ship took the six away,
All across the world to Botany Bay.
The six took a stand that was ethical,
Yet charged with swearing an oath illegal;
From Justice's sake it was a travesty
To become a workers' rights legacy.

Michael Vickery

The Yellow Bellies Of Lincolnshire

There is a spring mistiness in the air,
A yellow mellowness everywhere...

A crowd of daffodils dancing on the hills
Wild primroses in pale yellow
Cascading from high to low
Stars of selandine
Sparkling in woodland glade
Dandelions glowing in ditches and dips
Flowing carpets of cowslips and oxlips
The soft buttery yellow of a buttercup meadow
And the bold yellow gold of marsh marigold

Yellow, yellow everywhere
Everywhere I behold

But none compare to the full-on glare
Of oil seed rape of which the eye cannot escape
Bloated and consumed with this yellow bloom
Stretching out as far as the eye can see
A sea of yellow, as yellow as yellow can be

Skirting every lane and alley
Draping every hill and valley
Swathing every ripple and fold
Swelling every rolling belly
Of the Lincolnshire Wolds

Its seeds have taken root
In amongst the trees of fruit
In a church orchard of crab apple trees

For every year there reappears
A towering mass of yellow spears
Inching and pinching space from Queen Anne's lace

The yellow fingers of rape wrap around waste ground
Lingering around pockets of poppies
And where other wildflowers are usually found

Led along the water's edge of the riverbank ledge
Beds of rape have spread and now outflank the sedge

Every country road hedge overflows and glows
With the yellow rows of rapeseed wildly sowed
Fields of wheat, corn and maize are
Embroidered and laced into a yellow maze
Like a patchwork bedspread
Stitched with a single yellow thread

And even where cows mingle, graze and traipse
The seeds of rape disperse
And burst into a towering blaze
Like a pernicious weed or wildflower
There is no doubt it grows about
With such rapacious speed and tenacious power

Its tentacles spread like wildfire
Breeding, bleeding, feeding into every scene a yellow gleam
Like a trip into a mono yellow surreal dream
For crisps, cakes, curries, pastries, biscuits, bio fuel
Slow to boil, frying oil, cream and margarine

Jane Air

Full Board

This is the incentive: they can't get rid of me
if I show this much courage, doing it at last
in my sixties. Ideal aim: reverse redundancy.

Climaxes of walking the Pennine Way:
I survive Cross Fell in a mighty storm
and discover disorientation, that I can
use map and compass when GPS fails
see geology in the raw, join in,
as part of ongoing creation
get through a bog where Wainwright needed help,
put a fellow walker back together,
do it.

No accommodation at Kirk Yetholm
turns out trumps as I bus it to Edinburgh,
see Aunty Dolly still in her own home.

She dies soon after. To sleep over her bath
as I did as a kid: on wide duckboards.

Robert Shooter

Thank You

Last night she told me she loved me - for real
I listened to these words before
but I didn't believe them
But this time it was a genuine longing
I could see it in her eyes
Even amongst the drunken circus we were in
I knew it was real
and the words had waited to leave her lips for a long while
But you see,
As nice as these words sound
and as warm as they can make you feel
Does not make up for my absence of love
Absence of pure feeling
So to repay her genuinely
I didn't lie
Not to myself nor to her
I just drank down the rest of my whisky
Smiled
And said,
'Thank you.'

Zak Patrick Parsons

Thoughts

I thought about the world today, and what it means to me
Why are we here, what should we do, what are we meant
to be?
I didn't find the answer, but then I didn't think I would
And I wonder if my thinking really did me any good.

Why can't we all just live in peace, why do we go to war?
Why, when we have the things we need, do we always crave for
more?
Well I didn't find the answer, but then I didn't think I would
And I wonder if my thinking really did me any good.

Whoever created joy and love, created suffering too
Hunger, illness, torture, pain, can these be for me and you?
Well I didn't find the answer but I didn't think I would
And I wonder if my thinking really did me any good.

Just look at little children with their innocence of mind.
We're born with simple needs and wants, our way in life
to find.
I guess that is the answer, to think just like a child,
To try and be just happy, till our future's reconciled.

Graham Hayden

A Fledgling's Maiden Voyage

Please don't make me do it Mummy, I'm not ready for
this test,
why can't I just stay here in our comfy little nest?
I know the others have all done it I heard them chirping
with delight,
but what if I'm not like them and don't have a head
for heights?
From when I was an egg you have looked after me,
now you seriously want me to jump out of this tree!
I'm feeling quite confused and I don't know what to do,
please, please Mummy can I stay up here with you?
OK, if you insist I'll sit on this branch a bit,
then maybe if I watch the others I might get the hang of it.
Hey Mom did you just push me as I've fallen off the edge,
and now I seem to be clinging to a very tiny ledge!
Yes I know I have to do this but I'm afraid I cannot budge,
well if you insist will you give me a little nudge?
Geronimo I'm airborne I think it's time to open up my eyes,
oh I really can't believe this and it's such a big surprise.
Oh Mummy this is awesome in fact it's utter bliss,
I really can't believe that I was so afraid of this!

Catherine Wilson

Anorexia Trilogy - A Mother's Story

2006
So what to do when every bridge is crossed
and burned, and feelings trampled in the mud?
Is all that loving, caring wasted? Lost?
Are all the sacrifices so much crud?

I think the way I love you has to change;
your barbs have pierced my unprotected me;
my life, once yours, must now be rearranged;
I understand now, even love's not free;

not free to speak, to help when trouble looms.
To watch you hurting is my agony.
This is your choice? Cold silence? Empty rooms?
Then I must turn my back and walk away.

But if you miss the closeness we once shared
remember that your mother always cared.

2007
But no! I find I cannot walk away;
a moth towards a flame will make its track;
as hours drag and nights turn into day
my tortured dreams will always force me back.

However much you trample on my love
it does not die but simply cowers, bruised
and weeping, hopeless, gathering its nerve
till it returns, maligned and much abused;

but still an everlasting part of me,
it watches, waits and hopes to help in time,
someday to save you from this lunacy,
this dangerous and self-inflicted crime.

When all is lost and you must face your fear
just turn your head, you'll find I'll still be here.

2009
So finally your face is, once again,
the face so dear to me since you were born,
the hollow cheeks and shuttered eyes are gone,
you've made it through that savage deadly storm.

Once more we talk; I hope that we are friends,
together now we sometimes share a meal
but is this where the dreadful story ends?
I still doubt your recovery is real.

The spectre lingers ready to return
but, no my love, you dare not glance behind;
be vigilant; if only you could learn
to banish him forever from your mind.

I have you back but what has been the cost?
My daughter still but not the one I lost.

Valerie Sutton

An Unexpected Trip

She didn't know what to expect
As they drove up the winding hill road
their car pulled up and out she stepped,
The wind breathing against her ears

A playful breeze, ruffling her hair
She looked and looked again
before her the scenery was magnificent
The rolling, green Welsh hills

were spread out before her
tumbling into the valley, so far below
swaying and moaning the orchard trees groaned
the wind whistled, as the colour drained from the heavens

Car lights, bustled and moved in the far distance
Blinking in and out of sight
The cattle lowed peacefully as the stars appeared
Blissful, peace at last, a veritable feast for the senses.

Charlotte Ransley

A Man That Cooks

Last night
my darling husband
cooked dinner
again.
I was in bed
he brought it in
and fed it to me;
another cold bowl of lies
from the deceit kitchen
that sits on his neck.
My husband smelled like sweat
and a receptionist's breasts
but the first spoon tasted
like a busy workday, a traffic blockage
a flat tyre and a faulty jack spanner.

Tonight
I made him dinner.
His last.

Tolulope Akinyemi

Denim

Building up to this for weeks
I'd had my fill of online freaks
Writing to a girl so great
To finally embrace my fate.

Of course I knew her by her name
Agreed to meet me off the train
I said I'd wear a stripy shirt
She said she'd wear a denim skirt.

I thought I knew my Yorkshire well
At Castleford I nearly fell
Out of the train a nervous laugh
It really was an awful gaff.

There was no one to meet me there
All I did was stand and stare
Until a denim skirt appeared
And all the nightmares I had feared.

I thought of running there and then
The station held me in a pen
She shuffled near to where I stood
And stared and said, 'You're here, that's good.'

She suggested a hotel nearby
Where she could moan and shout and cry
And tell me all the things she'd done
With lots of menfolk on the run.

I suggested a quick drink instead
Where I could sit and hold my head
While she recounted sordid tales
Of men from Bristol, Leeds and Wales.

She said, 'Oh my, you drink a lot!'
I said, 'Oh yes, I clear forgot
My hobby's also drinking gins
And falling into wheelie bins.'

She said she'd see me to my train
In an hour she's back again
To meet another man it seemed
To help her moan and shout and scream.

A few days later in the paper
Apparently there'd been a caper
'Denim-skirted woman found
Strangled, wrists and ankles bound'.

Description matched this murderee
An online tryst that was the key
I sat and watched a ticking clock
And waited for the dreaded knock.

Gary Moss

Burning Castle In The Air

The castle in the air is burning to the ground. She cannot smile
any longer.
Another body. Another soul. An entire country beneath her heel.

Subconscious tidal waves are being pushed down. She cannot run
any further.
She feels their breaths. They are right behind her.

The sinkhole of the morning swallows them
when the cacophony of a new day temporarily saves her
from her soul's suppressed cry for help.

A distant scream that has been withheld from her ego
beneath the surface of her consciousness for so many years
that she doesn't know what's true or who she is anymore.

She stopped recognising her mirror image a long time ago.
That woman is far too old to match her ego which has not aged
as fast.
The wicks of the souls burn significantly longer than their shells.

The feeling of being one with her body is long gone.
The increasingly cracking and slower body,
but her holistic being feels increasingly connected to the spirit
world and the universe.
A humbling feeling of compassion for all human beings.

She finds it ignorant that certain individuals believe
that they are worth more than others and
unscrupulously rule other people's lives.

Ultimately we are parts of the same mechanism,
the same machinery - the same world.

A world we do not have the right to have at our disposal
because of our abundant needs, our drive to rule and the urge
for power.
We are all a part of the world we live in and the ground beneath
our feet.
Every step we take and every decision we make matter and
have consequences.
An enormous gear mechanism in an infinite machinery.

She escapes into a dream of freedom in which she flies.
Swimming through the clouds free from the weight of her body,
the fear of losing and the urge to win.
Her feet are off the ground and the wind strengthens her soul
before the tsunami of the truth forces her onto her knees.

The blindfold comes off and she beholds the essence of her soul.
She has to take important decisions for her inner harbour,
her country and her people.

When the heavy veil of self-deception comes off
the wings of the soul empower her entire body.

The liberating light of truth gives her new energy and strength
to make a difference and a revolutionary change for us all.

Eva J K Skarviken

Being Human

We are ruled by the longings of our soul
The needs of our being
The desires of our heart

We crave and we lust,
Feeling incomplete without our baubles and our trinkets
we hold on to them, to feel grounded.
To be human.

So numb to everything outside
our scope of understanding.
We focus on that one moment of immeasurable ecstasy
And we relive it
Over and over,
Wearing it thin in our minds because of our fear.
Fear of never experiencing it again,
Of our glory days becoming fond memories,
Warm blankets that shield us from the monotony of
our lives.

Temi Daike

Yesteryear

The songs and acts of yesteryear
With performances of a kind we hold so dear
Dancers, singers and they're acting too
Giving their best, to show for me and you
Jolsen the master who could do all three
His songs live forever, 'Mammy', 'California', and 'Climb upon my knee'
Then there was Jimmy Cagney, the man called to play the tough guy
But could he dance, rhyme, movement, tap, God he could fly
Jimmy Stewart the actor no one came near
Spectacular in the film 'What a Wonderful Life' which always brings a tear
Chaplin the king of silence, who made you believe
That in his films the underdog can always achieve
Lady Thespians, who were there also, to be loved and admired about
Dietrich, Mansfield, Hepburn and that sexy Marilyn Monroe's pout
I have not forgot Brando the actor we all loved to see
Especially with his masterful portrayal in the 'Godfather' films as Don Corleone
Just a few greats of the golden age for all of us too see, their show
They will never be far from our thoughts, as we will try hard not to let them go.

Philip Rugg

Appeal To Humanity

In this world we crave the things we see we want
To be so much more than we are
I just wake up each day and pray for those who don't have
a chance
The ones we forget or decide to feel some sympathy with
little thought
Of what really matters
Can you imagine life with little time
You wake up in the morning thanking God you have another
day spare
To cherish every second on this Earth.

Oh I just pray for those
I idealise their strength and admiration
For their recognisation
That our time is short and precious

And all the richer getting richer
And the poorer getting poorer
And the countries destroyed by war
Immigrants with no home or no luxury

Whilst next door only worries about how big their house is
Or how flash their car is
Darling, don't you think of the world outside your mind
Look around, destruction and chaos
Our world war is in fact ourselves with selfishness
When we lost humanity and forgot to help the underprivileged

Why does it take a terrorist attack to find some sense of humanity
of helping
When every second on this Earth we could be working together to
help one another
Peace has always won the war
But only when you work together
Share humanity, make it better
Let's find a way to right a wrong
Because the next bigger and better
Isn't going to change the realisation of the world
Until you turn around and find chaos has erupted and taken away
your beautiful homes and cars
And all that material had no worth
When it's gone but life has a price
The price to breathe and live every day
So precious so be kind, be wise
Bring peace not war and show humanity how human you are
For many do not have a choice
For those sick, disabled, poor homeless
The list is never-ending and some of these people's time is short
So why can they not have a luxury before leaving this Earth?
And some have no choice and things will never get better
But for who we are working or not working, healthy individuals
Who could show kindness
Be more because you want to
This is my appeal to wake humanity.

Danielle Harris

To The Tyrant

May you wake one moonless night
Alone in the dark to see and feel clearly
That you lord it over
A depleted dustbowl
Your people fled or damaged
Beyond repair
Your foreign funds dried up
Your land untended and unharvested
Your streams choked with dead things
Your weapons and threats become commonplace
Through overuse
Your reputation that of a spiteful thug
Your place in history becomes
A brief, shallow paragraph
Of summary and dismissal
Your memory welcome because you
Are but a footnote, a passing headline, a memory
Best forgotten.

Vivien Foster

My Mate Dave

My mate Dave, is just not the same...
He met this Italian girl and she's turned his brain!
These days he never comes down the pub for a pint.
Instead he drinks Prosecco and never has a late night.

And he's got one of those handbag dogs
To match his Italian shoes, which have replaced his clogs.
And we no longer go to cricket to watch Yorkshire play
I think he's been following Juventus these days.

For tea the other night he told me he had a 'frittata'!
Which followed the 'Bruschetta' he had for his starter.
Something 'nero' has replaced cabbage in his bubble and squeak.
And instead of Whitby, he's off to Tuscany for a week!

I really hope he'll still be my mate
... but I regret the day he fell in love with Maria Possellthwaite.

Kevan Taplin

Failed Conspiracies

In search of solitude
I go up my rooftop
Take in a large part of the icy breeze.
As I lift my eyes, my gaze fixates at something suspended
miraculously in the sky; surrounded and partly blanketed by
thick clouds -
It's the moon!
One of the most beautiful creations,
A masterpiece of the master,
The object of envy.

I am the moon
And the moon is me -
One of the most beautiful creations
A masterpiece of the master
And the object of envy.

The clouds, thick clouds surround me,
Overshadow me.
They think they can obstruct me.
Confine me.
Rob me of my marvel, my glory, my enlightenment.
They move closer to me.
Gang up to hide me,
Overpower me.

The dark ones fume with smoky wrath to overshadow me.
but they can't... it's all in vain.
My luminous beam pierces right through the heart of the
thickest cloud

Telling the world, 'I'm there!'
They can't hide me.
They can't stop me.

How ignorant!
How ignorant are they of the fact
That their effort to conceal me, in reality, reveals me.
I'm a plain-looking object otherwise.
Their conspiracies turn me into a beautiful spectacle
A breathtaking view
A cynosure!

The more you conceal me
The more you reveal me
Because I stand out
I stand tall
And I stand above all;
But above all...
I stand alone.

Delores James

Eclipse

An unpoetic day drifts by and
I wade into night in search of inspiration.

What is there to see?
A creative spectacle - Nature has really outdone
Herself - but I cannot write.

Tiny yellow-eyed stars, you dazzle and haunt.
Great black space, you enthral and engulf.
But blood-red moon, you devour me in your
Glory - my body, soul, and brain.

What mortal can scribble down such perfectly crafted
Majesty, already a Pulitzer-winning drama?
I am so painfully aware -
My spirit, my being, my craft are fatally
Eclipsed.

Olivia Gillespie

Do You Know Me?

I am so lonely, what can I do?
I know I mean nothing to you.
I bully my friends and kick and swear.
But if I was nice, would you care?

If I ran away, would you cry?
To look for me, would you try?
Why can't I be nice?
Why can't I be good?
Why can't I do as I should?

You want to know how I feel,
I can't live in a world that's real.
Deep inside I feel so scared,
Sometimes I wish that someone cared.
You may see me as someone wild.
But please remember, I'm just a child!

Susan Vowden

Lilibet

Well-behaved, sensible,
A jolly little girl.
Blue eyes, a pretty face.
blonde hair, with a curl
Orderly, responsible
with attitude and grace
She took the public stage.
At such a tender age.

Elizabeth Alexandra, Mary.
Elizabeth 'R'
A wife, a mother, a great-grandma.
Stands her ground, can play the clown
Has tact, knows when to frown.
Long may she reign, and wear the crown
With respect and pride, that's always been.
I wish to shout, 'God save our gracious Queen!'

Diane Ashman

Prize

I raced a silver moon last night
Minted in the midnight sky
From where it draped its watchful glow
Across the frosted plain below

And by its magisterial glide
It matched my stallion stride for stride
Tracing the track effortlessly
That I rode with such urgency

We shared that journey it and I
And more besides for as we vied
For mastery in that night-time trial
I saw its steel and it saw mine

And only then I came to know
I'd dare not race without its glow.

Peter Taylor

Tapestry

I unravel, skein by skein.
My first is a quadrant of skin.
The cells flake, and shed.
Under a microscope, I am light.

The second is golden thread.
Look twice to appreciate its brilliance.
In places, dust dulls its texture,
dissolving when smoothed.

My third is luminous,
an aura around my heart,
a crystalline diamond diadem,
white pearl and lit coral.

My fourth requires patience.
Unweave me - please.

Sarah Safraz

Poem A Day

A poem a day seems easy to achieve
Life after all is every day
A groggy call
On my back I slide forth
The day I see as my blur snaily slimes my eyes
The room where the sun shines in
The water flows quick and life is alive again
Head down to the bigger realm
Organs livened
That I know there is more than
That I am just small
That I must...
Walk through the grog of another
Blessed grey haze
And
Get gaily on.

Ashley A Burnside

The Smilers

Don't get ideas above your station.
Art, you say? Such a fanciful notion
Is not fit for modern times.
And reading fiction?
A middle-class hobby,
Nothing more.
Back in the day, when we were at school,
All was regimented,
Straight and true.
We knew just where we stood.
We learned our Latin declensions
Then hurried home
For tea and crumpets
Beside a roaring fire,
While our nannies poured us
Nice warm baths.
We weren't required to
'Express ourselves',
'Explore our creativity'.
No, we made do with abacus beads.
We knew our maths, of course,
Soon learned to look at balance sheets
And throw aside all that was
Not required.
We did not venerate great ideas
Or individuality.
Instead we learned to rule by stealth.
We cast aside all thought of magic.
Saw instead a chance to hide

Behind pale masks of smiling calm.
Education?
We had the best
And yet, you say, learned nothing.
So, listen well,
We'll strip the system bare
Until it's like the thing we had:
An empty, awkward silent thing
Reserved for those who wear the masks,
Who understand that boats
Should never be rocked.
And dreams? Don't make us laugh.
This is not a world for dreams.
This is our world.
Tread carefully when you step in here.

Philip Caveney

The Greatest Painting

With closed eyes and deepest thoughts
In awesome wonder perceived
The greatest painting ever to unfold
With skill arrange this masterpiece
The artist at his easel paints
The creator on his throne creates
Love, beauty, knowledge, understanding
Kindness, forgiveness, guidance and togetherness
With invisible hands flowing brush
The expanded artwork was created
Its creative beauty is indestructible
It never dies; it's reformed throughout the years
With fiery explosions it has been tried
To destroy the concept that exists in man's dreams
The co-ordinated strokes bend to his will
Contoured, shades from dark to light
Adding striking colours, the masterpiece progressed
A canopy for cover, with a sun to heat and light the days
With moon and twinkling stars to illuminate the nights
A rainbow and living, ever-drifting clouds
Unimaginable beauty as the mixture slowly unfolds
Of striking bold and gentle shades
The story of the greatest creation was designed
The green of the grasses blend with the leaves
Of every size and density, flowing as one unit
The multitude of fragrances to delight the senses
Skilfully mixed the patched work earth glazed
A brilliant rainbow within the canopy formed
This done the living waters break and foamed

And rivers gently meander undisturbed
This panoramic beauty never dies
It retreats into seasonal slumber
Waiting to greet another glorious spring
To bring forth its beauty and charm
The painting continues its reproductive cycle
By the unseen magic of the invisible hand
A work of art recreating and restoring
This continuous masterpiece that is never finished
It's an ongoing productive creative piece of art
The master creator and designer breath-kissed the Earth
And granted this, his everlasting creation of beauty
The greatest painting ever created.

Burgess Jay Barrow

Life As A Girl

So
If I am a virgin
Let me get this right
I'm a prude
But also 'tight' and desirable

And if I sleep around
As free choice dictates I can
I am called a slut
Unlike a man

If I take pride in my appearance
I'm a high-maintenance job
But if I am more relaxed
I'm a slob

If I wear hair extensions and fake nails
I'm trying too hard because natural is best
But the girls wearing no make-up
Get less attention than the rest

Be confident, that's sexy
Don't forget to speak your mind
But not that much you're annoying
Make sure you're feisty but kind

Boys like the chase
So don't be that easy
But don't make him wait too long
Or you're a tease

A skinny waist is preferable
But, oh wait, not that skinny you twat
Gain some weight
But, oh not that much, now you're fat

You've got spots
Don't you wash?
You're wearing too much make-up
Oh my gosh

How can I ever win
When I'm judged before I'm even in?

Victoria Sands

The Orange Girl

'Oranges! Oranges! One and nine,' she did sing in the limelight's
shine,
From stalls to boards, in a dress divine, lips red in desire,
Wandering along stall by stall, her skirts, teasing 10 a time
Passing notes from merchants to trade, smiling sweet
and divine,

Never to pass a want or repose, from a duke or merchant for a
guinea or two
Hoping and waiting for her prince to come, to take her from this
hall,
and she waits by theatre's flanks, deaf to whistles and boos,
Looking in the stalls with limelight bright, before the
curtain falls

Still with youth sweet to her face, her charms for all
who pay,
Talking in song to all the gents, with eyes open and
deeply wide,
the final curtain falls heavy and a gent to escort her away,
tomorrow she'll be selling oranges, red-lipped from the side.

Gregory McDowell

Bright Red Poppies

The poppy bud hangs her somnolent Morpheus head,
Like Demeter when the loss filled her with dread.
The petals unfurl baring their soul to the sky,
Their vibrant colour brightening everything nearby.
The velvet touch of the soft silken petal,
Holds the look of tissue, fragile and special.
The blood-red poppies stand out amidst the field,
Looking so strong, standing tall, unprepared to yield.
But on its own a poppy falls and straggles unsupported,
As a monarch without an army, soon to be thwarted.
But the vibrant colourful poppy also brings light
and brightness,
Filling the world with hope, and illuminating the darkness.
Like the strong forward thinking memories of a
hero's lament,
Knowing the sacrifices he would make, will be well spent.

Gillian Garwood

The Bench

Walking along a path I come to a bench,
Nothing special,
Just a wooden bench,
Sometimes with somebody sitting on it,
More often not,
I have known this bench for many years,
It has been there
Long before I first knew it.
Just overlooking the hill
Into the valley below.
The faded and rubbed plaque
Is still there,
But all you can see is a date,
Nineteen thirty-four,
And the name Fred.
Who was Fred?
Was this his place of contemplation
So many years ago?
Dreaming his dreams,
Thinking his thoughts,
Sitting and watching his life,
As it meandered past,
Like the stream in the valley below.

I wonder what life it has seen
In all those years?
People of all ages,
Just sitting here thinking.
Couples together in a loving embrace,

Others drinking and eating.
People laughing.
Others crying.
So much of human life
Will have been seen by the bench,
Even mine.
As I sit on it,
I am lost in my own and nature's world.
Sometimes writing words,
As these words are being written,
While sitting on the bench.

Andy Brister

Decarnivore

Sparks of fire light your
Fantasy, and you sigh
In your sleep because
Dreams ignite your mind
With untamed sensuality.

The pillow a place so
Seeped with unfulfilled
Greed that the forgotten world
Or dormant desires percolates
Your day with a burning itch.

And they are like a coffee
Shot to your system that
Wakes you up from a
Transient state, and suddenly
Your focus is on one spot -

Him - his electric eyes
Gazing so slow that
Paralyse you with ecstasy
And you're left searching the
Reason he is so captivating.

A touch like a hot blue
Flame that makes your
Heart beat loud and your
Skin tingle and drives you
So happy, so insane.

Escalations and heart
Palpitations in a dark
Blind room filled with
Moans and remnants of
Intense flirtations.

Lust leaking from our
Pores and the blood-red
Feeling of kisses on our
Skin like invisible tattoos.
We are Scorpio carnivores.

Paulina Bawiec

Portmanteau

Dissipate your condensation
Over lingering duration
Electrically seeding skies
Let yourself go and the mind flies.
High above the gates of Heaven
Strings controlling allegations,
Covered from beyond afar
Managing radiant solar
Energy manipulated,
Sinister the beast.
Chemically deliberated
Secretly released
Deeper into the stratosphere
The proof is all too far from here.
No scientific evidence.
A single morph that represents
The federal declaration
Of persistent condensation
Unfavoured evaluation
When they acknowledged existence,
Such a powerful resistance.
The blame was rarely hard to find
When Occam's Razor sprang to mind,
Reminding one fewest is best
The vapour's been put to the fucking test!
How could commercial pilots be
The pawns of space controversy?
The righteous in a war unknown
A secret plot to kill their own?

Test agents on the populace?
Breathe in the air,
relax,
embrace,
For deadly spraying has no proof
Your destination holds the truth.
So buckle down, pay attention,
There may be more they hadn't mentioned,
And if reports live up to the buzz
It's safe to know they're killing us.

David Dixon

Flavours Of An Alley

Opposite houses stooped with the burden of age
Nevertheless lean forward to confer and gossip

Dwellings spill out their copious innards:
Glorious cornucopias overflowing with flea-ridden fruit
Hung out to ripen by day, keep cool by night

Hung too are lines of clothes
Criss-crossing the shady passage
Their frowns intensifying as they wrinkle and dry

And on baking rooftops
Red chillies wither and die
Commencing a respectable, sun-kissed afterlife.

Swati Gupta

Looking Back

Dark and dismal?
No, bright and sunny.
Wet and damp?
No, dry and airy -
Or so it seemed, looking back.
Optimism saw in the year.
It came in bright and breezy -
Or so it seemed, looking back.
Then darkness and long shadows came
With shorter days and nights -
Or so it seemed, looking back.
But no! Along came light and laughter
Brightness and cheer -
Or so it seemed, looking back.

Pat Salisbury-Ridley

My Grandad

My grandad is my hero
He helped me be myself
He wouldn't let me fail
Or put myself on the shelf

I remember lots of things
That he taught me how to do
Clean a pair of glasses
A shiny toe on a polished shoe

He helped me drive a boat one day
Then let me do it all
Until, that is, the moment
I nearly hit the harbour wall!

Each year we would go to visit
And go down to the beach
But the stone I threw hit Grandad's head
Because the sea? It didn't reach.

I loved his mashed potato
It was always smooth and creamy
With Grandma's steamed meat pudding
It really was quite dreamy.

I had an accident one year
A visit to A & E
But he never left my side
He really looked after me.

When we went into the town
Grandad had a points system
Especially with a pushchair
He'd shout and plough right through them

I made so many memories
Each summer I went to stay
My thoughts of my amazing Grandad
Will never go away.

Shelley Foreman

Vanity

Three hours in front of mirror, mirror
at the crack of dawn
clearly weren't enough
to Coco channel your fears and self-doubts;
to mask your insecurities and revitalise your conceit
beneath more bronze layers
than are found in the crust of the Earth;
to stop you running from the naked truth
that promises to strip away the façade, expose the masquerade,
undress the pretence
of your fragile, self-endorsed image
that fails to factor in the maximum cost of the haughtiness
you esteem to laud over everyone and everything;
to stop you sitting, incessantly obsessed and absorbed
by the small, reflective square
clutched possessively, protectively
in splotchy, unnaturally tanned fingers.
An arsenal of products is painstakingly applied
to erase the worry lines
induced by a life of little more than maybes;
to hide the high-maintenance, sallow complexion, sagging mouth
Sunken eyes and crow's feet
the stress of keeping up appearances
has laden you with at the grand old age
of thirteen and a half.
Admiring the reflection that smacks
of Paris, New York or London City
you plant an idolising kiss on it, only to leave behind
residue of the priceless lipstick
worth more to you than love, education or friendship.

It is frantically retrieved and reapplied
to activate the endless cycle: Apply. Kiss. Repeat
the adoration, the worship of a visage
that knows nothing but its own petulant, desperate demands.
Such a shame that for all the effort put into that face
it represents perpetually, eternally, absolutely
nothing. I hope you think you're worth it.

Simon Day

She Dances - Stes-Maries De-La-Mer 1966

She dances
Dances on eggshells
Coloured eggshells
Tell me
How
I can pass her by
Without stopping to watch
And she's dancing
Dancing
By the light of candles
Lamps
As the gypsy men
Stand shouting
Cheering
Clapping
While she taps and stamps the ground
She's dancing on eggshells
Hands held high above her head
Spinning, stamping, screaming
Like the dance
The music
Was her fight for breath
O she dances on eggshells
Arms outstretched
Snapping her fingers like castanets
As the gypsy men shout
And clap her on

Tell me
Why
Would I want to walk by
And not stop
And watch her
Dancing
On coloured eggshells
For them.

David Satherley

Amor Vincit Omnia...

If I am here when you have gone; if I am left behind alone -
I shall remember our last kiss, each detail of exquisite bliss.
If you should leave without a word, I'll still remember all I heard,
Recalling all you ever said in memories I thought were dead.

If on your pillow is a space where I once saw your sleeping face,
Then I shall feel a poet's rage who gazes at an empty page
When inspiration's run its course, when nothing and no one
can force
Creation into vibrant life - destroyed by sorrow's wilful knife.

I'll feel an amputation pain - the limb excised, yet still remains
The aching of a part new gone from that which now is
quite alone...
If I am here while time rolls by, and in the silence hear your sigh,
I shall remember prayers we prayed when in a church our vows
we made.

I shall remember how we broke those vows, and yet we
never spoke
But once of leaving; love is strong, and love is right, though sin
was wrong.
I shall remember what you gave, and how you loved me to
the grave;
I shall remember what you took, recall your every loving look.

I shall remember love is all, and overcome the numbing thrall
Of grief; then, having shed my tears, recall how you would quell
my fears...

If you are free whilst I am bound to roll with Time its daily round,
Then I must find the strength to cope, and in that strength
recover hope.

If I am here when you have gone, if I am left behind alone -
I'll briefly taste grief's bitter gall - and then find peace -
Love conquering all.

Jenny Proom

Flying North (May 14th 2016)

The Flying Scotsman tears through Cramlington Station
With cries of hurray and a sense of elation
She speeds through our lives with the thunder of steam
Cuts through the air with the help of slipstream
Resplendent in colour, of National Railway green
Polished by her crew to a lustrous sheen.

She's taken on water at Heaton Depot
For her journey to Scotland, she's got far to go
The people she passes all take her photograph
The news of her coming on bush telegraph
They'll never forget this moment in life
Forgetful of bills, and government strife.

Picking up speed, she streaks for the heather
Flashing through Morpeth, it's all hell-for-leather
The driver has got the throttle full on
As Edinburgh's promised the end of the song
Acklington, Alnmouth and Chathill too
All witness the toil of the hard-working crew.

To Berwick and Dunbar, she flies like a swan
Taking on water from track troughs along
People are waving from houses she passes
Sheep look on puzzled, while munching on grasses
Soon she approaches Waverley Junction
In a great cloud of steam, she ceases her function.

From King's Cross through York and Newcastle was the mission
Edinburgh's reached through powerful piston's unison
The crew can relax with a pint and a meal
Steeling themselves for return journey's zeal
Until then, they wearily climb from the train
In three days' time they'll be doing it all over again.

Adrian McRobb

The Old Rocking Chair

The old rocking chair,
Was swaying to and fro,
Outside on the porch,
The day we said hello.

That chair would groan,
Under both of our weights,
That's how we ended,
The majority of our dates.

Before that rocking chair,
I bent on one knee,
Asking my soulmate,
If they would marry me.

In that rocking chair,
Our children you would feed,
Sometimes late at night,
You would just simply read.

The chair came inside,
As sunshine turned to rain,
The gentle rocking motion,
Seemed to ease your pain.

That chair and I,
Went to hell and back,
The day you sat,
Dead, from a heart attack.

The old rocking chair,
Meant so much to you,
Also the next generation,
Our grandchildren love it too.

Phil Brooks

Yule

Tangle us into the boughs of the trees
Redden our cheeks with the sting of the breeze
Tie up our hair in red ribbons and lace
And dance our way down to the magical place
Where the spirits of yule and of midwinter sing
For the promise and hopes that the coming months bring
Watch the sparks billow out as we race round the fire
See the shadows join hands as the flames ascend higher
The wine that we spill is our gift to the Earth
And we spin and we sing now for all that it's worth
Then exhausted we sleep 'neath the mystical night
And the madness of winter sleeps on till next light.

Tia-Louise Way

Even Today

How long had we been waiting
for fate to bring us two loners together?
And who knew? Certainly I didn't,
that we'd be bound to each other forever.

How long before I noticed
that there was beauty, and sadness, in your eyes?
I saw it, surely a reflection;
a sign that meant so much more than I realised.

Even today you still move me that way.
I wish you could hold me.
Even today, with our lives unfolding.

How long have we been talking,
never able to say what we're feeling?
Existing, largely in our own worlds,
discussing everything but the real meaning.

Even today I don't know how I stay
silently asking.
Even today, with so much time passing.

How long - can you remember,
have we been friends with this strange understanding?
While loving, though we never said it,
embracing all that the future was planning.

Even today you must know that I pray
that we could relive things.
Even today it would make a difference.

Peter Stephenson

Angel Of Modernity

A slow but furious flame, flickering within the darkness of
enchanted imaginations.
Forbidden flirtations, passionate and persuasive in their
translucent lucidity and longevity.

The tenderness of touch, of thought in which the fever of illicit
amour raging with a love so strong,
stronger than anything that wants to pull one back from
attempting to move forward.
A closed book? An embrace without affection?
A weakness that transcends and traverses the very depths of
one's seduced, secretive and yet tortured soul.
A collection of thoughts and wishes of desires... of carnal desires.

If only to intrude upon the thoughts of the 'other', the self,
modernity herself in mischievous, malevolence of a love that can
never truly materialise.
To seduce this adorable, phosphorescent, spectral, angel would be
to win the hearts of the God's themselves and yet as idyllic,
beautiful and elegant as this dream is sensory the intrigue of this
adulation has no end.

The dream is but a continuum of life itself, a never-ending story in
which the ending can't be foretold.

Anthony Bryce

A Siberian Story

Igor Popopkin had his very worst fright
On the day that the landslide
Carved away the hillside
For there in the ground was a big
Hairy
Animal
All fierce with tusks.

The mammoth
Poor thing!
Had his life truncated
When the Ice Age came
And his world glaciated
His state of perfect preservation
Was due to deep refrigeration.

But Igor
He knew none of that
He thought
Hairy!
In the hole
Must be a mole
And might, one day
Come up beneath him
And jolly well eat him!

And Igor
Didn't fancy that
So he ran
And he ran
Until he was far, far away.

Lionel Etherington

My Cricket That Never Worked

Our task for that lesson
was to bring our crickets to life.
How clever, I thought
And as the etching dissolved the unwanted copper
We began to snip away the parts:
the bulbous creamed ceramic, covering the wire
as each resister I put down in neat identifying piles
of coloured banding, all bee and body-shaped.
The diodes, though smaller, were my favourite colouring
and the smell of solder to me was almost comforting
like my grandfather's old garage
its lead and tin mix made me wonder
would we become mad as hatters

some of my classmates appeared close to the edge of
somewhere...

With most practical projects mine remained hopelessly silent
While, with amazement, I watched as the other fellows
Would cup theirs in their hands and wait or else
Leave them in a dark, quiet cupboard somewhere and wait
Where, after a while, they began to chirp away nicely.
My suspicion arose with inadequacy,
I began to wonder whether some Masonic secret had missed
me out.
A gift, perhaps, handed down by some elusive alien species
whose DNA had not reached me.

My cricket
that never worked
where are you now?

Brad Evans

Disillusioned

See the pretty girl with her vodka and Coke
Sitting in the dingy pub with the same sad bloke
Wishing her life was better than this junk
Sat watching footie in a pub full of drunks

In another life she would have been admired
Wined and dined and passions she'd have fired
I pray she escapes from her lacklustre life
And doesn't end up an unfulfilled wife

I hope all her dreams come to fruition
And she is able to fulfil any burning ambition
She shouldn't be a lost lonely soul
Digging herself into lethargy's hole

Once I was contented, happy with my lot
Sunshine in my veins, an overflowing pot
Dark clouds then gathered and hovered overhead
Harmony and peace drifted into dread

Now I feel as empty as a drained wine glass
Thrown and forgotten. Placed in the past
Silent tears flow like a black and white film
Indifference creeping feasts like a bad dream

Life doesn't make you sad it is there for you to live
People make you sad, taking from you all that you can give
Love doesn't break your heart, it's a gift to celebrate
People break your heart as they chip at it with hate.

Cheryl Vallely

The Greek Meze

The Greek Meze is a most sumptuous feast
Which will fill any appetite
Starter dips Taramasalata, Tzatziki and Houmous
With hot pitta bread as you enjoy each bite

Halloumi cheese with Lunza bacon
Garlic mushrooms and Spicy sausage
Well-presented dishes come one by one
Waiters careful to avoid any damage

An array of fish will come your way
Calamari, Whitebait and Cuttlefish too
Red Mullet or Sea Bream freshly caught
From the Mediterranean Sea so blue

Spinach in pastry and Stuffed Vine Leaves
Filled with tasty mince and rice
Healthy Greek salad and Feta cheese
Yes it really is that nice

Kebabs of chicken, lamb or pork
Their appealing aroma lingers on
Kleftiko, Stifado or Afelia to enjoy
Don't rush and you'll have no indigestion

Don't forget to choose your favourite wine
St Panteleimon for me and water is OK
When you've tried it once you'll want it again
You'll never tire of the Greek Meze.

Andrew Evzona

G-Arden

The world is such a huge place;
Today I'm concentrating on my little garden space.
A tree stands proudly in the corner
At its base is a rockery, the stones are differently stacked upon each other,
Colours blue, green and white are flecked by the reflection of the sun.

The grass is patchy with hues of brown and yellow,
Leaves are scattered in various stages of life...
Embedded in the safety of the earth.

I cast my eye up to the sky,
A blue dome with white clouds that drift on by:
My ears are listening to the different sounds
That echo round and round and round...

I hear the wind softly blowing a breeze,
Through the trees' leaves which flutter and spin,
Delirious at being in a sudden tease,
Then freeze to seize a stronghold before being allowed
To fall down, down...
Abseiling to the ground without a sound...

Silence...
Then a bird chirps up, another answers,
And a cacophony arises -
I love listening to these natural surprises.

Darren Halladay

The Reformation

Lap, lap the water, a continuous lapping
Throughout the night
Above all it is the sound
Of water lapping that remains in her memory

A recollection of that exhausting journey
Will remain forever imprinted
In her mind, an expensive dream
Huddled together, in a small boat
Money for old rope
A small fortune, the price of freedom
How can they remain true
To the sound of shelling and gunfire
When there is no future in staying

Mother West will be kind and fruitful
In her offerings, a place of sanctuary
A new beginning, strange tongues
Strange tastes, cold nights, cold days

Lap, lap the waters
She lies in the bath
Her first for months, on the island
Mother West has provided
Lap, lap the water
As she dreams of her homeland
And yearns to be there.

Agnes Brookes

My Dream Pet

He is my best friend
Always there
A silent support

He is my best friend
By my side
A loyal presence

He is my best friend
Standing up for me
A fierce protector

He is my best friend
Leading me through darkness
A constant guide

He is my best friend
Saving me
A brave rescuer

He is my best friend
Laughing with me
An enthusiastic playmate

He is my best friend
My family
My dream pet.

Ruth Miser

Forever Fallen

She came willingly, the girl who was their salvation. She gave
Bray's hand a gentle squeeze. As if he wasn't leading her to
slaughter.
The colony gathered. The corridor they formed was a waxen,
twisted thing, lines of men and women whose skin had shrunk
over their bones and split into black, festering maws. Each daubed
a spot of blood onto the girl's forehead; when she reached the
island's centre, the child's face was dark from hairline to nose.
Marcella waited, scythe in hand. The girl slit her palm on the blade
and her own blood joined the smear on her brow. She curtseyed
and climbed up onto the dais.
'This is not the way of things,' Marcella noted, voice low.
'She is different,' Bray acknowledged. 'I have never seen a tithe so
calm. But that need not be a bad thing.'
When the moon was fullest, the girl stood. 'Awake,' she said,
'arise. Or be forever fallen.'
Marcella removed her head with one stroke. There was a
discernible beat; then the colony descended, withered arms
outstretched to claim their portion.
They gorged until the sun beat down on newly distended bellies.
They gorged and fell where they stood, sated and spent.
By the close of day, the sleeping figures had been transformed,
rejuvenated by the ritual, healthy and whole.
The island's scavengers feasted for weeks on the colony's fatted
remains. When the moon completed its cycle, a girl stood amongst
them, her ruined face split by a smile.

Jennifer O'Gorman

October Gold

If we care to listen, there's a whisper going about,
a gentle sigh borne on the wind, the land is breathing out.
Faint echoes of the summer drifting gradually away,
replaced by scents of woodsmoke, earthy leaf-mould and decay.
Wind-tossed painted leaves lie thick upon the ground
hiding dormant chrysalids and beech masts can be found
beneath tall trees whose burnished leaves - responding
to the cold -
are tinted now with copper, bronze, and subtle shades of gold.

Song thrush sings precarious on windswept autumn twigs,
attached to rain-soaked branches dancing wind-lashed
autumn jigs.
Rosebay rise through leaves aflame, gold capsules twisty-turny,
ripe seeds in silky parachutes begin their autumn journey.
Pale honey-golden grass stems and acorns plump and mellow,
Campion's golden goblets, small birch leaves butter-yellow.
These gilded ghosts of summer - such ingenious creation,
providing sculptured backdrop for quiet thought and inspiration.

Sparkling dew-kissed spider's web ties knapweed stems together,
festooned with madly spinning leaf, white thistledown and feather.
Copper carpets rotting now, returning to the earth,
sustaining ancient oak trees with their furrowed, ample girth.
Toss misty morns and rainbows in a frosted mixing bowl,
add a frisky wind as flavouring to elevate the soul.

Janet Vernon

The Scream

It's androgenous, it's ageless, it is raceless, it is crude;
It is stark, it is real, it is terror in the nude.

It's the Herodean mother of an infant son,
It's a passenger in an aeroplane on 9/11;
It's a woman who's fallen into the hands of Fred and
Rosemary West,
It's the patient lying helpless with Savile's hand upon her breast.

It is Auschwitz, it is Guernica, it's a Christian in Iran,
It's the Spanish Inquisition, it's the dreaded Taliban.
It's somebody held at knifepoint, it's a battered wife or child;
It's a murder victim's relative, it's a woman forcibly defiled.

It is Hurricane Katrina, it's an earthquake, it's a flood;
It's the Boxing Day tsunami, it's the Egyptian river of blood.
It's the mistral, it's a bush fire, it's the Titanic hitting ice;
It's Vesuvius, it's quicksand, it is lightning striking twice.

It's a nightmare, it's a flashback,
It's untreated mental illness.
It's a bombing raid, a gunshot,
An explosion in the stillness.

It's androgenous, it's raceless, it is ageless, it is crude,
It is stark, it is real, it is terror in the nude.

Kathy Rawstron

The Broken Man

The broken man
The dying man
In the quiet room
Blue dim light
Searches thoughts
His silent thoughts
His shrilled and troubled
Breathing thoughts.

His fears, his dying tears
His loves, his hates
His now meaningless fates
In this towering hour
His last and final hour
Will his tears freeze?
Troubled breathing rests
In his rising chest?

What can he fear here
More than the life he lives?
Death's falling gown
The echo of life's fading sound
The broken man
The dying man
In the quiet room
A blue dim light.

Norman Dickson

Memories Of A Schoolgirl

The worn leather satchel bears
the weight of sixteen years;
a phone of dated photos;
a diary of lost events;
a key to a house once lived in.
The smell of dried ink, and spilt drinks;
the scribbles of experience, marked
in a small notebook resting on a
fractured watch at the bottom.

Hannah Derbyshire

Growth

The way you move, sinuous and free,
Like a breeze twisting through leaves,
Our legs and arms entangled,
Like the boughs of the strongest trees,
Entwined, solid and resilient,
Persistent through all weather,
Our vines growing up through one another,
Each shoot another part of our story,
Binding us closely together,
Until our strands are indistinguishable,
And they cannot be told apart,
Overgrown, enclosed and safe,
With enough light and space,
To allow new shoots to burst from the earth,
Which weave and grow with the old,
Blooming into strong upward pillars,
To hold us up, adding to our ever-growing tapestry,
That tells the tales of us.

Nights spent taking root in each other's souls
Some mornings spent embedded in misunderstandings,
Only to be expelled for us to grow again,
Robust, unbroken and beautiful;
Like the boughs of the strongest trees.

Alex Oleksy

May I

May I never lower myself
To hate any of mankind
May I never inflict pain
No matter how well deserved
May the Lord guide me
To rise above mediocrity
And aim for the stars
May I emulate those I admire
But never lose my identity
May I smile at a stranger
For that smile may make a difference
May I overcome fear
And experience life
May my word be my bond
No matter how fickle the creature I face
May my love be all-enduring
Even in the face of adversity
May I learn from hardship
But not allow it to tarnish me
May I find someone special
Who celebrates my glory
May I have the strength
To be a rainbow
In someone else's cloud

Asma Khatun

Sergeant Bill

Where are you lying now, my Sergeant Bill?
They sent me back your letters, Sergeant Bill
Sent me caps and sent a kitbag
Sent me boxes and a bold flag
But no one thought to send me Sergeant Bill

Shipped you off like cargo, Sergeant Bill
Stamped and documented, Sergeant Bill
Gave you boots and gave you Blanco
An old rifle and some ammo
But no quartermaster gave me Sergeant Bill

Where are you lying now, my Sergeant Bill?
Telegrams forgot to say, my Sergeant Bill
Said how proud they were and grateful
Great deeds you did, but fatal
But paper's not the same as Sergeant Bill

I suppose you did your duty, Sergeant Bill
Still I'd rather have a coward, Sergeant Bill
To hold me and to need me
To love me and to feed me
Through all the years you leave me, Sergeant Bill.

Nigel Mellor

Harry The Ant

Harry was a wayward ant,
Who never did what he was told,
Yet all the other ants
Believed that he was bold.
He liked to climb the highest trees,
Just because he could,
Even though all the birds and bees
Said he never should.
Harry went to a school,
For ants who misbehave,
But he told all his friends
That it was because he was brave.
Harry missed the school bus,
Due to being on detention,
A fact that to his parents
He somehow forgot to mention.
His dad had rung the school,
To find out why he was late,
When Harry was finally let out,
His dad was waiting at the school gate.
Once home he learned his fate,
Ten minutes upon the naughty step
And no more sitting up at night till eight.

Pauline Uprichard

You Need Someone

You need someone to love you before you fall apart
To care for you forever with all of their heart.
You need someone to live for, someone to live for you
To be there in the bad times to help you make it through.
You need someone to be special because of who you are
Someone to understand you and not push things too far.
You need someone to think about, who can make you smile,
Make you be all happy and ponder for a while.
You need someone to live with you, to wake up by your side
To sleep with you inside your arms and lovingly confide.
You need someone to kiss you so you can kiss them back
Someone to be beside you and keep your life on track.
You need someone to show them how much you are in love
Someone to be intimate with, not someone to shove.
You need someone to give you a better chance in life
To make you mean something and maybe be your wife.
You need someone to be a part of the things to come
To be there when you're sad and when you're looking glum.
You need someone to treasure the things that matter more
Someone to be your partner, someone to adore.
You need someone to dwell with and hope it can be me
Because you truly love me and want us to be free.

Nicola Penistone

City Dreaming

There is a room full of a million painted faces,
Sweet potions; fragranced footsteps dancing in the dark -
Multicoloured raindrops, with city lights burning bright.
New delights are discovered,
Like silk ribbons swimming down moonlit alleys -
Chalky shadows, in the dappled shades of London night.
It ripples off my fingertips; I mould each corner like clay,
Each turn holding no burden but treasure.
Yet where is the ocean of your heart?
Every songstress of the night can sing,
But cannot yield to the sweet stories,
Which fall from your mouth like music onto a page.
And these naked forms,
They bear a shallow resemblance to water -
A transparency;
So cold to the touch.
Through an apocalypse I see your shadow dancing,
And off the walls that contain these figures -
Only your story I hear.
Their orchestra of chaos has flown;
Leaving,
Only you.

Victoria McAnerney

Unknown Face

Flicking through old photos, I come across a face
It's one I don't recognise, one I just can't place

Black and white pictures, weathered and torn with age
A face so proud and serene, stands out from within
the page

Your name and memory has been lost over the years
No one to love or mourn you, for that I shed a tear

I wonder what your life was like, how you spent your day
Where you lived and what you did, I'll never know your ways

I trawl through old records, a clue I try to find
As to who you are, and the life you left behind

Piece by piece, your life slowly unfolds
Just waiting to be discovered, a story to be told

And then one day, everything just falls into place
And finally I can put a name to what was that
unknown face.

Becky Bishop

Big Brother

Oh my gosh it can't be
That's not white hair I can see
Oh my gosh no you haven't
Cut off your sister's plaits
Oh my gosh you've cut them off
Left her with two little tufts
'Lully told me,' is what he said
'Mummy stick them to her head.'

Kerri Madders

For The Distance

To me, love was like a sprint.
So my heart
learnt to beat quickly,
chaotically,
like it was running away.
You showed me love was for the distance, and
you're training me to beat strong and steady because
Love is stamina.

Christabel Samuel

Mother Of The Groom

Mother of the groom
It all came around too soon
That little boy with grazed knees
Whom you cuddled, kissed and squeezed
You crooned him to sleep each and every night
He who never wanted you out of his sight
As he grew, the prouder you became
He began school and life was never the same
His adventurous journey had begun
You were after all a testament to his fun
Later, as he left his boyhood behind
You watched from a distance the friends that he made
You worried at times when old ones began to fade
But he was your boy, his intentions would always be good
He matured, travelled, did good deeds, you knew he would
You now observe his love for his child so gentle and kind
That, my dear friend, is the love that we weave and bind
Be happy and joyous on his wedding day, tears may fall
As he and his bride pass by, be so proud, you can walk tall
Because you gave him a wonderful beginning and life
Now it is up to him to do the same for his child and his wife.

Vivienne Doncaster

This Love

It's hard work, but it's a natural progression,
To make the transition from a low to high,
But when you get it you will know the reason why,
So take the chance and nurture it like a flower,
Use it and control the amazing power,

It's so precious, never take it for granted,
It's what you have always wanted,
Some you may leave with a push or shove,

But you will know it's genuine and it's called true love,
It can be easy or sometimes hard,
But the feeling's unique when Cupid's dealt you that card,
From your eyes to the tips of your toes,
There is nothing quite like 'the love' that grows,
But the hurt you feel when that love goes,
So keep it safe and secure, that love you have for evermore,
In the end remember the start,
The seeds of love began in your heart.
So make your heart the thing you follow,
Because losing the love makes it bitter to swallow.

Lee Blunt

The Burn Of Love

The burn of love, scalds from deep within
Leaving no trace or marks on my skin
It's a pain like never felt before
Leaving me broken, a bundle on the floor

Made me believe every word that you said
As soon as it gets serious, you turn and fled
The tears leave tracks stained on my cheek
A damaged soul who's lost and weak

I gave you all the love that I had
You ruined me, made me angry and sad
Telling me that I still mean so much to you
How can I believe a word you say is true?

My love for you was all too real
It didn't come easy to tell you how I feel
Medicine doesn't cure a broken heart
Here I am right back at the start...

Broken.

Laura Aimee

Festival

Lying spread-eagled
across several fields
the giant slowly wakes.

From his humid canvas pockets slither,
Lilliputian campers, yawning whither,
blinking eyes, pupils' dilation,
cool relief from precipitation.

Surveying the resting Gulliver's torso,
like apocalyptic zombies, only more so,
bedraggled, hungover, barbed wire heads,
guy-lines secure his canvas threads.

Tiptoeing around his muddy pores,
and debris left from last night's scores,
past parasitic neon burger vans,
selling local stodge and global brands.

to his muffled bass-bin heartbeat thump,
our heavy feet plod but our spirits jump.

Rob Dunsford

The Bus Conductor

With beetling eyebrows black and bushy
And eyes that bore right through your soul
He grudgingly takes my proffered bus far
Hurtling the coins into a bowl
The terror of the northern counties
The children daren't move or stir
And if anyone whispers a conversation
He'd hear, no matter how quiet you were
He'd walk between the aisles, his cap
At a menacing angle, his features grim
And even the most rebellious schoolboys
Never dared say a word to him
He'd come towards you, an evil grin
On his glaring face, you stare quickly down
The sweets that you bought, are still in your pocket
Saved now till the safety of the town
He puts the fear of God in those
Who are on his bus and his reputation
For cracking the whip is legendary
And he does it with pride, till our destination.

Tanya Silva

Moss Eccles Tarn

(For Beatrix Potter's birthday.)

She saw geese landing
on its silvered surface,
wings skimming
over liquid hills and trees.

She gazed at
fish circles in the water,
frogs with fishing rods
in her mind.

'Once upon a time... '

She walked this terrain,
the young woman with a sketch book,
a snow-mountained distance
backdropping the quiet;

caught the sky
in a rabbit's coat.

Paul Mein

The Spider, The Snake And The Man!

I can kill a man with just one bite.
I can kill a man with just one bite and watchhim shudder and vomit.
I can wrap him in silk and watch him suffocate.
I can wrap my coils round him and watch him turn purple.
I can shoot him, gas him, stab him, drown him, choke him,
Break his mind and blow him up,
Said 'the man'.

Sheffphil

Human Cry

I see it in the light,
the light of my very soul.
It shines upon my wandering way
yet gives no hope.
Hopelessly I drift with
saddened heart.
I am as nothing.
Should never feel as those
who feel. Could never cry the
words that carry me.
Did never look with brightened eyes
at future clouds.
I am as nothing.
To lose them all I lose myself,
disguised within the human race.
No strength to hold but break apart
in pieces.
I am as nothing.

Felicity Milne

Bibliophiles

When I within your four library walls
Did engage with several books awhile
Your winsome glance, once read, did me enthral
And my heart ensnared was by that smile.

While your look spoke to me in rich volumes
Little did I realise so much then
How my heart would surrender 'mid your tomes
That love is much mightier than the pen.

New chapters were well-written in my mind
With every visit read between each line
I yearned in spirit with your soul to bind
And wished with all my heart that you were mine.

What would I not in some novel time give
To know that in your hands my tale would live.

Denis Bruce

Rose Red

To me alone, you are that red, red rose
Blood-red deep velvet, so soft to the touch
The one whose perfect perfume fills my nose
Whose beauty is profound, unique as such

Standing elegantly erect, all alone
With your face raised bravely towards the sun
So you have nothing at all to atone
For you know, you will always be the one

Pick you gently I must and be so bold
Hold you close without any of your scorn
All I want is your beauty to behold
So I must look out for your prickly thorns

Holding you now, in the palm of my hand
Now you know, now I know, now we understand.

Barbara Coward

Learning To Cook

I fear that my hand might burn
But I am determined to learn

Cut the onion with a sharp knife
My mum says, 'It's about time you moved on in life'

Wait for the onion to turn brown
Then slow the heat down

Add the chillies in the pan
Try to be strong as much as I can

My eyes water and my hand shakes
But I will complete this no matter how long it takes

I add the chicken and wait for it to cook
It's so easy I didn't even need a recipe book.

Sonya Hussain

You Used To...

You used to tell me that you loved me.
It made me feel ten feet tall.
You used to tell me that you loved me.
It made me feel I could break down walls.
Now...
You used to tell me that you loved me.

Brian Weston

Deep Appreciation

Deep appreciation
No words can express
My deepest gratitude
For all you mean to me
On reflection of my life
From the day we first met
You have been my rock
In a multitude of ways
Physically and emotionally
Psychologically and spiritually
In a word holistically
But words only glimpse
At feelings I can't convey
Of that gift God sent to me
That weary September day.

Maura Guerin

Harness Of Time

Harness of time reigns Pegasus stars shine,
Whose rising shews now spurs the Sothic star,
Across the heavens in pole's plough align,
On rowed sea's course of pharaoh and great Ra.
So moving's arc ascends in starry glow,
To Nile life's reed boat the journey's skies,
While blaze of this dog star ere belt suns row,
Now guide sons in an orbit which stares eyes,
And draws a draft in silence through the night,
Like passages in pharaoh's cryptic rest,
Where he is bound to sail in in-verse light,
To heaven's sound Osiris' gold zest.
Thus time does wind its course in light's oared space,
And with these man-gods do Eternal race!

Barry Bradshaigh

Fading Lights

Arms raised we charge like the Light Brigade: on
And on, into the arms of the waiting
Tide. No thought of what lies ahead, nor gone,
Just the now, the wash of water tracing
Lines into the sand, as if by being
Here somehow we can begin again to
Wish like children, across the stars, seeing
Everything in nothing - the waves run through
Our fingers, like the storm that is about
To pierce the very soul of us, the rope
That kept our hope bound with our fear and doubt,
That caged us, aged us, rises up to choke -
Arms raised we charge like the Light Brigade: on
Into the ocean, where our time has gone.

Victoria Penn

Not Quite New York

Manchester's skyline sang a haunting lullaby,
As I watched the city switch off to sleep.
The commotion of the world came to a halt,
Whilst I slipped through the silk of the night.

The darkness regurgitated from the graveyard,
As the moon hung preciously like a china plate.
The stars appeared, as the windows of Heaven,
Whilst the pale street lights were put to shame.

The starry-eyed mortals disturb the peace;
Chanting football profanities into the night.
I look above me and gaze at skyscrapers,
As a lethargic New York slowly falls asleep.

Abigail Quigley

Plane

Look at the aeroplane up in the sky
Me! Oh my, watch it fly
In and out the clouds it goes
Like an eagle, it just soars

London, Paris, New York City
In and out the clouds so pretty
Thunder, lightning, rain or storm
Flying is all the norm

Passengers are all in their seats
Air hostess comes around and hands out treats
The pilot reports that the weather is good
But, do stay seated if you could

Audrey D'souza

Arachnid Horror

A roving city of spiders
Rustling legs in shadow
In doorways, behind curtains
Scurrying, dusty and watchful

Static sparks across the carpet
Bristled energy in measured bursts
Eyes unflinching with insect desire
A woven silver web awaits

The looming arachnid horror
Tangled in hysterical frenzy
Eight legs approach from below
The helpless quarry liquified.

Wayne Barrow

The Higher Ground

She was indeed in the crater, talking as usual. She chopped her hand through the air the way she did when she was making a point. Next to her, sitting on the stump of a fallen birch, was a blonde giant. Even from his sitting position he was taller than she was, looking like a Viking crossed with the drummer from a heavy metal band.

The Worry Hamster - which had now set up home again - began to pace around in his stomach. If it came to a fight he'd be dead. His only option would be to outrun him. The Viking-looking man adjusted his ponytail. As he did so, he switched the gun between his hands and Mark quickly reappraised his position. Even if he tried to outrun him he'd be dead if the guy could shoot in a straight line.

He watched them for a moment and debated his next move when he heard a cracking sound from a couple of feet to his left.

The bough he was standing on began to snap. It opened up beneath him like a pale mouth. He quickly took a step towards the trunk. He glanced in the direction of the crater but saw that Sadie and the Viking man had spotted him in the tree.

He instinctively put his hands out to steady himself. The branch recoiled as he redistributed his weight. His wife and her kidnapper watched with open mouths as he was gently lowered towards them.

Adam Cook

Autumn's Grace

Autumn holds no platter bare
or golden chalice unfulfilled,
such wine to fall upon your lips
and tasty morsels resting there.
Disappointment has no place
within this maiden's hand.
For when the winds do turn their face
her graces fall unto the land.
In her heart such secrets hid
all promise there to keep.
When comes the dying of the year
her tender eye shall weep.

sweetwater

Rose Petal Tales - An Extract

Chapter III - The Cooking Pot

To find where this story takes place, you have to be lost. And here you are. Ivy slides up the crooked walls of the cottage, as though a land-kraken is slowly dragging it down, engulfing it for supper. Its dish is served with a garnish of exquisite garden. Daffodils trumpet, forget-me-nots giggle, pansies gossip, tulips flirt, (vetch tuts at that) and bold peonies in bunched burlesque feathers boast over them all. Dandelions sneak into the smallest spaces and try to look inconspicuous. Fat carrots, rhubarbs, parsnips, cabbages, runner beans and marrows all wriggle themselves into the earth as deep as possible, trying to drown out the racket of the flowers and not think about the pot. Herbs artfully spin their scents into the air; dizzy lavender to calm, prickly rosemary to entice, soft jasmine to welcome, clever thyme to confuse and fennel like the Green Man's whiskers. A tousled rhododendron bubbles over the wall, its dark magenta flowers fearless and seductive.

The gate is ajar.

Yet vegetable leaves stretch to hide the path; they know you should fear the pot as much as they do. But, oh, little one, aren't you tempted? Breathe in that incredible scent. Let it snake over your body, plunge into your belly, tiptoe in and out of your pores. Isn't it just... just... Just look at that maybe-open gate... If you are very careful, you could steal in. Just for a spell. But you mustn't let Her catch you peeking... eyes are Her favourite thing to chew.

Holly Thwaites-Bee

In Salem

A dark night
A crowd gathering
A woman misjudged

Ropes that bind innocent hands around wood too thick to break

Fire...

Screams...

Witchcraft they said.

Natalie Denvir

A Silent Gasp

I stare at her lifeless body lying there, seeing the soul drain from her eyes. I reach out to touch the smooth skin of her hand, it feels warm and suddenly I drop it and back away.

She's lying on the bed, her pale skin a stark contrast to the dark silky sheets, pooling around her limbs like blood. Her blue eyes follow me wherever I move, like an eerie painting. I know if I turn away I'll feel her stare on the back of my neck, cold and prickly like frozen fingertips.

My brain seems to kick into motion slowly, willing me to walk away. As I turn, I glance through the window into the dark, inky night and at that moment a security light blinks on. I see her watching me, her mouth forming a silent gasp. I panic, catching a glimpse of my reflection in an ornate, patterned mirror on the wall. I start as I see the strands of hair that must have caught on my watch and now cling to my clammy skin, feeling like they're crawling up my wrist.

I turn quickly, not noticing how my foot pulls at the bed clothes. I walk fast towards the door, only jerked back to stark reality as I stumble over the letter, the page crumpling underfoot as my stomach churns with nausea and dread. The letter had simply said: 'It's yours'.

Gemma Roman

True Love

Your skin is slowly turning pale, the red glow that once brightened your cheeks is ebbing away. The bright eyes that filled the room are now dull and vacant, yet the final moments of your life are still etched on your face. The warmness of your lips still entices my fingertips, but I know that will fade soon. My hand caresses your chest for the once strong beat of your heart but nothing acknowledges my touch.

Silk flowers of your dress scrunch in my tight-fisted grip with tears dripping over your perfect form. You were my future, we were to get married, have kids and buy a house together. All that has now gone.

Red sickly liquid mats your hair. I try to wipe the blood away but it spreads covering my fingers and disguising your beautiful face in a twisted scene of horror.

If only you had listened to me and not spoken to that man. I knew he would do this. You had to keep talking to him and sending messages to him. He led you astray, corrupting you. It is his fault this has happened, not mine. He will pay for this. You were mine, no one else's. Now no one will have you. This was the only way I could stop you leaving me. I will see you soon, my love. He will suffer for this.

James Elworthy

Finding Balance

If you live in the past you're robbed of your future
If you live in the future you're robbed of your present
If you live in the present you're robbed of both your future and
your past
If you live in the moment of your emotion you might just find
peace and balance between them all.

Ross Mitchell

Things That Look Like Mistakes

Fake mistakes all over the place in paintings. A bright smear
where it shouldn't be, jam on a child's face. Anomalies. Clues to
make gasps in hushed galleries.
Dances too, a stumble melts. Bone-free bird, will she fall, will he
catch her, will she burst on the ground?
A pause in Act Two, Scene Three of 'A Rose in Autumn'.
'Do you think you'll ever marry, Lady Catherine?'
Should be quick, should be, 'I think not, my dear,' snapped out like,
'None of that nonsense.'
Young wisp playing Emily turns rose-pink herself, flustered, is she
counting seconds of silence? Counting on you, and the crowd
all wait, expectant, then think you've forgotten your line, then
each feel certain they know Lady Catherine's secret.
And her, 'I think not, my dear,' is understood
all the more perfectly.

Lizzy Huitson

Reaching The End

In loving memory of my nan; Patricia Cooper (1929-2016) who enjoyed poetry more than anyone I knew.

The sun is setting in your world
And soon, will no longer rise again
I can't stay until the darkness
As the sunset brings me to tears

You may soon no longer have sunrises
But I hope there's no storms in your days
I also hope you find peace in the night
And that you have stars to pave the way

Rebecca Nadin

Star Gazing

I see the constellations in the spring
My hopes get brighter
Constellations in summer glory shed
Deepest winter stars of hope

They tell me where I am
I remember Venus there
That time when things were bad
But here I am still star gazing.

Pam Mills

Eight O'Clock

He woke, roused by the half-hour chime of the steeple clock; but half-past what? Had he really wasted the night sleeping? As he sat up, he heard a faint sound of horseshoes and iron-rimmed wheels on cobbles then, except for the rustling of his mattress, it went quiet again.

He swung his bare feet to the flagstone floor. He wouldn't need boots again and had traded them for a wool blanket and a fresh filling of mattress straw. That had been a mistake. If he hadn't been so comfortable he might have stayed awake.

The three-quarter chime came and went then, at last, the hour chime and after a pause the deeper tones of the hour bell. But he knew the time now without counting them as, during the chimes, a door had clanged. Breakfast was on its way; it must be seven o'clock.

He hoped he would be able to eat it - they would all watch to see if he did.

As he ate, the sounds of an awakening town punctuated by the relentless clock chimes filtered through the narrow barred window.

No one spoke until the time came for the walk across the courtyard. He hoped his lack of boots wouldn't make him falter on the cobblestones as they escorted him towards the timber stair. Pride in the exactness of their timing would let him hear the steeple clock chimes.

But would he hear the first stroke of its hour bell?

Tom Robertson

Little Shadow

Oshiro Takashi hadn't known what to expect when he ventured into Tobokami, but it wasn't this. The wealthy noble was surrounded by squalor and filth. Half-naked children ran riot between derelict squats, weaving in and out of the legs of disgruntled adults. Rough-looking teenagers squared up against one another, their audience chanting for blood as trinkets exchanged hands between seedy-looking gamblers. The smell was rancid, and as he approached, he realised that sewage was running freely into the river.

The same river in which toddlers were lolling and scooping up water to quench their thirst. Where wizened old men were hooking up fishing lines; hauling in nets with barely any yield. Where gossiping women and girls were rinsing through rags of clothing, singing jauntily: a small boy stealing away with scraps of material, taking them to a merchant in the hope of swapping them for a half-mouldy persimmon.

Takashi hadn't known what to expect, but it was clear that he intimidated the inhabitants as they retreated, staring at him with a mixture of awe and respect, fear and loathing. He wondered if they treated all Reapers the same, or had his life in the house Oshiro made him that bit more impressive?

Sayuri had come from here. His beloved wife. Her delicate, fleeting beauty. Her humility. Her fragility. Her struggles. Her pain. Her guilt. All from this pit of despair.

Takashi hadn't known what to expect but he now knew he feared what truths the past might unearth.

Victoria Bunting

Wet Haddock Man

'Well, it's not the end of the world,' my father would cheerfully declare upon receiving a hefty electricity bill.

'Better than a slap in the guts with a wet haddock,' would be my mother's verdict, standing, hands on hips, regarding another flat tyre on our accident-prone car.

These two phrases served as the leitmotif of my childhood.

'It's not the end of the world,' my father consoled me when his father, my obese grandfather, sat down upon my violin, crushing the life from it. I took up the descant recorder instead - aurally just as painful.

'Better than a slap in the guts with a wet haddock,' said my mother when our pet dog, Molybdenum (Mo for short), mistook my recorder for a bone and gnawed it with such relish that it snapped in two.

Years later, my father's world ended and my mother sank into the pit of Alzheimer's - a fate worse than any haddock-in-the-gut experience. I took to carrying my old violin case around with me, within it a whole fresh haddock. (I had a standing order with the local fishmonger.) Whenever I came upon anyone extravagantly moaning and groaning about anything, I'd open the case, whip out the haddock, hold it by the tail and give a good thwack at the abdominal region of the complainer. *Thwack!* No words were necessary. The thwack always conveyed the required message. Thus I became Wet Haddock Man, the upholder of optimism in a dismal world.

Steve Leighton

Holding My Breath

I wait in Mother's bedroom, holding my breath; it is contained in a jar labelled 'April's Last Breath'. I study it carefully, trying to remember the moment this wispy, fragile ball of gas was exhaled from my body. I draw up my shoulders, open my lungs and take in a gulp. As I shrink back, sighing out the air, I focus on how my chest feels as it closes in. But it's different now. I know in that last moment, the contents of this jar were gasped for, longed for and ached for.

After death, the act of breathing is optional. I can't recreate the racing heartbeat when I have no beating heart. I can't hope for the invigorating sense of air filling my body, then feeling the blood pumping from head to toe. I can't hope because I know. All that feeling, the sense of living that fearing death gave me in that moment, was the very moment being alive was taken from me forever. I walk over to the old oak dresser that had fascinated me as a child, but repulsed me now.

Carefully, I replace the jar in one of the cupboards of macabre miscellanies. Whereas other parents, showing pride in their children, display to the world an array of photographs and sentimental knick-knacks, my mother's secretive cabinet of curiosities is intended for her eyes only. It wasn't full yet. The lives of her first five children are (can I say celebrated?), are documented within the cupboard.

Liz Rich

Cucumber Confusion

Growing up, most children wish to become astronauts or footballers or pop stars. But for Adrian Swift, this was certainly not the case. When Adrian Swift was a lad, all he ever wanted to do was grow cucumbers. Now I know what you're thinking: *How odd! Why would a little boy be so obsessed with growing cucumbers?* Well, Adrian Swift came from a long line of cucumber enthusiasts. His grandfather, Albert Swift, was cucumber mad! And his father, Ronald Swift, was in the 'Guinness World Book of Records' for growing the world's largest cucumber. So at the age of forty, can you imagine how happy Adrian was when it was announced that his home village would be holding a cucumber-growing competition!

When the big day arrived, Adrian was so excited he could barely stand still. He knew for a fact that his glorious cucumber was a cut above the rest! He sniggered as he surveyed the other pathetic attempts at cucumber growing. So as the cucumber judges looked at each entry, jotting down notes onto a piece of paper, Adrian perfected his winner's speech in his head. This was his moment of glory.

When the judges finally arrived at Adrian's competition entry, Adrian was about ready to burst with elation! The first judge picked up Adrian's entry, looked at it for a brief moment and said, 'This is a courgette.'

'I'm sorry?' said Adrian, baffled.

'This is not a cucumber,' replied the judge, 'this is a courgette.'
And that was the end of that...

Tom Moody

Man On A Mission

It's not often the morning dog walks become the stuff of drama, but today was different.

It all started when a silver Land Rover tore into the train station car park, the roof leaning heavily as he rounded the corner at a speed usually reserved for motorways. Whipping past, it blew dust into our eyes. I commented to my pup that perhaps his hair was on fire; I could think of little else that would warrant such urgency. My baby Labrador was unimpressed and we carried on with our circuit.

Seconds later, two things happened: a train pulled to the station overhead and the driver of the Rover, a tall, thin man pounded up the pavement with his suit coat flapping. His Oxfords were a blur as he sprinted for the stairs with the wild look of a scarecrow taking flight. Had he even had time to find a parking spot or had the vehicle simply been abandoned?

I silently wished him luck. It was a long flight of stairs but he had the air of a man with a demon riding his shoulder.

Was he a banker? A lawyer? On his way to his first job interview? Or late for his own wedding?

I will never know if it was a mission impossible. The only thing I do know is, it wasn't a secret any more.

Cheryl Drenth Baker

The Dagger And The Serpent

I am the dagger the serpent entwines. I am the heart that owns the soul. Claim my soul, take my light as our shadows embrace. Entwine my purple heart. I am the staff whose rifts were healed by the strong hand that has clasped my soul.

He is the soul-shaker, the Devil may cry. My heart has been won by the silent one. The key to the throne, the key to my besotted heart. He is the soul-shaker, the heart-taker, the barbed wire ripped away from my crushing heart. The rose so young has become the rose betrothed. To the magical, mythical one.

Red for danger, red for passion. Pink for the truest of loves cast amongst the shadows. As we embraced under the stars so bright. Longevity of love. The dark is my smile, the emerald in my eye. The breath to my voice, the light in my heart. The love that perfected my life.

My life once a crown of thorns, now a golden hue. Beset by the deepest sunset on the longest night. A solstice of love, an ethereal dream. Surreal and sun-kissed but dark like the mist. Cold and eerie. But as joyous as the first call of spring.

The reaper of love, the reaper of my heart an immortal love. An eternity forever together as in the tombs of old. A story of love, a noble heart that has reaped my once solitary soul. The dagger and the serpent which entwined, forever together a clasp-like hold.

Amanda Jayne Gilmer

The Ritual

The old man knew that it was mid-morning because he could just see the sun glowing dully behind the thick blanket tacked across the window. His eyes could no longer take the day's full brightness. He wondered if it was time yet and outside a cat stopped at the window sill, sniffed, tail quivering then fled silently on. It was very quiet.

His leg began to twitch, first just a little then more until, with an effort, he lifted it with his hand an inch to the side and it stopped. The sound of his breathing, rasping now and again, began to worry him. Oh, oh - when would he come?

Two streets away, the boy hung precariously on the edge of the tramcar, a dangerous game they always played but no one had been hurt yet. The tram rocked and its wheels screamed as it took the curve where the street narrowed.

There was a very little cry when the side of the truck hit the boy and the driver wept as he protested he couldn't possibly have seen him. The sirens wailed their Te Deum. The old man shivered as he heard them and the clock struck eleven. The old man wept. When the woman came who fed him and washed him, he was lying there quite still and the tears were dry on his cheeks. It was very quiet.

Shropoet

South Of The Border

The procession sets out at dawn and rambles along the littered bank of yellow grass by Highway 45. Though the night is long and noisy, pierced by screams and gunshots, the dawn is always a fresh start. The walkers wave at passing cars, dance with each other, commune openly with a force or being only they can see. Every saguaro cactus is a listening post. Here in the desert they speak in liquid tongues as the morning light sweetens and deepens.

Some of the motorists are frightened by the apparition of this otherworldly parade, but others know them well and wave back and honk. These early morning pilgrims feel safe on the outskirts of a border town where death is as regular as rain is in the north. The journey always leads them back to the concrete walls and iron doors where it began – their prison, their refuge, their asylum. But each time they set out it is a new beginning, and at each step along the way there is a chance for something unexpected to reveal itself.

There is always hope. For some, the most urgent hope is that they will make it through another night, and not succumb to the embrace of Our Lady of the Shadows. But for others, that embrace is precisely what they most desire. In the company of Our Lady there will be no memory, no pain, no hectoring voices – no need for another morning walk.

Fern Bryant

In Praise Of The Hunt

Picture the scene: a bright, cold Boxing Day morning. The huntsmen and women assemble before the manor house, bright in scarlet - which, illogically, they refer to as pink - or sober in black. Their polished mounts are excited, dancing from foot to foot, snuffing the chill air expectantly. A butler hands round a silver tray: steaming cups of punch or cool, elegant tulips of sherry.

Then the master sounds his horn - they are off! The hounds are a flurry of waving tails and questing mouths. Away over the countryside they speed, galloping across fields, flying over hedges, the frost scattering brightly under their horses' hooves.

They have given the quarry a sporting head start. He is agile and clever, dodging round trees, turning back on himself, splashing down streams to put the hounds off the scent. But the hounds are clever too, and much faster. Soon, all too soon, they run him down.

He turns at bay, his back to the gnarled trunk of an old oak. The hounds fling themselves upon him, eager for their reward. Laughing, he digs into the pocket of his jacket for the expected treats, scatters them to the waiting hounds. 'You got me!' he says.

Patricia Feinberg Stoner

Novel Extract: Out Of The Goldfish Bowl

It all comes down to this one moment, consciousness filled up to overflowing with only one thing: the big, bright light. Two giant suns, bleaching my retinas, excluding all else in a terrible blindness. White-hot light coming towards me. Far too fast, too fast to brake, too fast to swerve: it's already too late. I give in to the overwhelming feeling of powerlessness.

Everything goes from slow motion replay to fast forward: all things happening at once. The furious sound of metal hitting metal. The reverberation and vibration, inseparable, juddering through me, right to the marrow. The windscreen explodes and a million diamond bullets sparkle in the white of the headlights, flying towards me, my arms go up in front of my face as the outside world smashes its way in.

The front of the car folds like tin foil origami and something big is torn from its very heart. The pain resembles a religious experience, exquisite and outer body. It hits hard, pushing me beyond anything I can stand, and further. A white supernova exploding ever outwards, stronger and brighter with each pulse. The stars are falling, crying out of the sky in streams of silver tears. I blink with my one clear eye. The dandelion halo of the street lights explodes in orange sparks that smudge the blackness of the night sky. Everything has lost its surface, sharply defined edges blur and merge, coming together in a blanket of colours: badly stitched and frayed at the edges.

Tony Northover

The Last Crematorium In Sussex

A jolt wakes Jordan Ferguson from his deep sleep. He knocks his phone to the carpeted floor and panics, until the LED light appears and shines in his 40-year-old, well-maintained bearded face. He flicks through his apps and there it is - the voice recorder. He verbalises, 'Chg chg wah wah chg', and lays down languidly as he got that sound out before it dissipated. The sound is a guitar riff, a guitar riff to change the world. Only problem is, Jordan cannot play and currently lives in a zombie apocalypse.

It's now 6:43am and Jordan checks the camera he installed before the days the undead ruled Sussex. The buzzer is pushed by a dark-skinned man with long grey dreads and a weary beard. A machete stained with blood drips from his right hand and he holds a wooden cart in his left. Jordan opens the gate.

He is the fishmonger from the High street. Clarence is his name, this man once of a huge family, but not anymore. 'Fergus,' Clarence says in a London accent, 'Please take care of my loved ones.' Fergus looks at the cart which holds three recently turned members of Earth. He nods. Clarence holds out a black sack of canned fruit, and spaghetti Os as payment. Out of respect for their past lives the zombie slayers of Sussex brings their dead to Jordan, as Jordan is the last funeral director in Sussex with a working crematorium.

Mark Wincott

Light

It's in the sun, as it bites through the clouds and spills onto the grass, that I feel the strangest. The sun lights up other people's skin, pink and dark and fleshy. Fragile human bodies. The sun illuminates us, tells us that we all have a skeleton, a heart pushing blood through our limbs. I look at all the separate bodies, walking, breathing and navigating the Earth with their feet on the ground and instantly my own breathing seems so real.

Or, I'll feel strange when I peer through a train window. I'll feel uneasy, seeing so many houses pass by me, never knowing who's in them, them not knowing me; it's unsettling, to live as an ant in a nest, so tiny. I live in a row of houses just like them; I'm a miniscule figure out of the window of a train, my house a box, a toy house full of ants, faceless and nameless. I'm a figure through a window too, a half second blur, someone else's insignificance. I vanish just the same. I'm an instant and a stranger, never seen again or never seen at all. Like a ghost.

I thought these things alone, on the train; but, when I'm with you I feel as I do in the sun. It's like I'm in the sunlight, as though my skeleton and my blood vessels are on display. Lamp-lit. You've always been like that, lighting up my insides. You're full of fire.

Josephine Dowswell

Untitled

It was dark, not the sort of empty dark that you get out in the open at night, but the all-encompassing, close, claustrophobic dark. That's the only way I knew I was inside. I reached out to my left and felt a cold, metallic surface, it was smooth and unyielding. I could feel the same sort of texture behind me through the thick jumper I'd been put in. I knew it wasn't mine as it smelt unfamiliar, like stale cigarettes and mustiness. I tried to stretch my legs out in front of me but could only get my knees to a right angle bend before reaching another wall, this one made a more wood-like noise as I knocked against it while my right side was again another metallic material. I discovered this by shuffling a little and reaching out to that side until I came into contact with the cool surface. The right side was slightly different, however, as there was a small groove running from top to bottom down the centre, like two panels that would draw together or maybe lift up, only they wouldn't move no matter how hard I pushed or hit it. The top was made of the same wooden material as the side in front of me and the base was made of the metallic material, cold seeping through the trousers. I wasn't sure if these were mine or not, they felt familiar but without being able to see I had no idea.

Ceri Amber Clark

Everyone Suffers

Life is hard, people dying because of every type of hunger, everyone suffers, dreams lost in the visions of success, everyone suffers. Greediness creating frustrations and confrontations, everyone suffers, judgements with decisions of wars and pain, everyone suffers, pollutions and explosions spreading negative signals to each and every human. The children are competing, mimicking their parents, trying to be dominant, while some become champions, others become losers. The games create a contest. Who is really number one? The people who try their best or the ones who don't have success? Everyone suffers. When will the gatherings come back to the central and go out to each and every outer point? The former lives are as important as the modern lives. Everyone suffers. Life is hard, people dying because of every type of hunger, everyone suffers.

Limbani Nhlane

FORWARD POETRY INFORMATION

We hope you have enjoyed reading this book - and that you will continue to enjoy it in the coming years.

For free poetry workshops please visit **www.forwardpoetry.co.uk.** Here you can also join our online writing community 'FP Social' and subscribe to our monthly newsletter.

Alternatively, if you would like to order further copies of this book or any of our other titles, then please give us a call or log onto our website.

Forward Poetry Information
Remus House
Coltsfoot Drive
Peterborough
PE2 9BF

(01733) 890099